Baja California

las nubes, rocas enormes que no pesan,
los montes como cielos desplomados,
la manada de árboles bebiendo en el arroyo,
todos están ahí, dichosos en su estar,
frente a nosotros que no estamos,

Baja
California

WITH LINES FROM OCTAVIO PAZ

Translated by MURIEL RUKEYSER

and the Geography of Hope

PHOTOGRAPHS BY ELIOT PORTER   TEXT BY JOSEPH WOOD KRUTCH

EDITED BY KENNETH BROWER   FOREWORD BY DAVID BROWER

SIERRA CLUB · SAN FRANCISCO

For all the usual recreational purposes, the alpine and forest wilder-
nesses are obviously the most important, both as genetic banks and as
beauty spots. But for the spiritual renewal, the recognition of identity, the
birth of awe, other kinds will serve every bit as well. Perhaps, because they
are less friendly to life, more abstractly non-human, they will serve even
better. On our Saskatchewan prairie, the nearest neighbor was four miles
away, and at night we saw only two lights on all the dark rounding earth.
. . . A prairie like that, one big enough to carry the eye clear to the sinking,
rounding horizon, can be as lonely and grand and simple in its forms as the
sea. It is as good a place as any for the wilderness experience to happen; the
vanishing prairie is as worth preserving for the wilderness idea as the alpine
forests.

So are great reaches of our western deserts, scarred somewhat by prospec-
tors but otherwise open, beautiful, waiting, close to whatever God you
want to see in them. . . . In that desert climate the dozer and jeep tracks
will not soon melt back into the earth, but the country has a way of making
the scars insignificant. It is a lovely and terrible wilderness, such a wilderness as Christ and the prophets went out into; harshly and beautifully
colored, broken and worn until its bones are exposed, its great sky without
a smudge or taint from Technocracy, and in hidden corners and pockets
under its cliffs the sudden poetry of springs. Save a piece of country like
that intact, and it does not matter in the slightest that only a few people
every year will go into it. That is precisely its value. Roads would be a
desecration, crowds would ruin it. But those who haven't the strength or
youth to go into it and live with it can still drive up onto the shoulder of
the Aquarius Plateau and simply sit and look. They can look two hundred
miles, clear into Colorado; and looking down over the cliffs and canyons
of the San Rafael Swell and the Robbers' Roost they can also look as
deeply into themselves as anywhere I know. And if they can't even get to
the places on the Aquarius where the present roads will carry them, they
can simply contemplate the *idea*, take pleasure in the fact that such a time-
less and uncontrolled part of earth is still there.

These are some of the things wilderness can do for us. That is the reason
we need to put into effect, for its preservation, some other principle than
the principles of exploitation or usefulness or even recreation. We simply
need that wild country available to us, even if we never do more than drive
to its edge and look in. For it can be a means of reassuring ourselves of our
sanity as creatures, a part of the geography of hope.

—Wallace Stegner

We gratefully acknowledge permission to reprint material from the following
books by Joseph Wood Krutch:

The Best of Two Worlds, copyright © 1950, 1951, 1953 by Joseph Wood
Krutch. Published by William Sloane Associates. Reprinted by permission of
William Morrow and Company, Inc.

The Desert Year, copyright © 1952 by Joseph Wood Krutch. Published by
William Sloane Associates. Reprinted by permission of William Morrow and
Company, Inc.

The Forgotten Peninsula, copyright © 1961 by Joseph Wood Krutch. Published
by William Sloane Associates. Reprinted by permission of William Morrow
and Company, Inc.

Grand Canyon, copyright © 1957, 1958 by Joseph Wood Krutch. Published
by William Sloane Associates. Reprinted by permission of William Morrow
and Company, Inc. In Apollo paperback edition.

The Great Chain of Life, copyright © 1956. Reprinted by permission of
Houghton Mifflin Company, Boston.

Henry David Thoreau, copyright © 1948 by William Sloane Associates. Reprinted by permission of William Morrow and Company, Inc.

Human Nature and the Human Condition, © copyright 1959 by Joseph Wood
Krutch. Reprinted by permission of Random House, Inc.

More Lives Than One, copyright © 1962 by Joseph Wood Krutch. Published
by William Sloane Associates. Reprinted by permission of William Morrow
and Company, Inc.

The Twelve Seasons, copyright © 1949 by Joseph Wood Krutch. Published by
William Sloane Associates. Reprinted by permission of William Morrow and
Company, Inc. In Apollo paperback edition.

The Voice of the Desert, copyright © 1954, 1955 by Joseph Wood Krutch.
Published by William Sloane Associates. Reprinted by permission of William
Morrow and Company, Inc.

We are also grateful for permission to reprint poems from *Selected Poems of
Octavio Paz*, translated by Muriel Rukeyser. Copyright © 1963 by Octavio
Paz and Muriel Rukeyser. Reprinted by permission of Indiana University Press.

Photograph previous page: Boogums blooming near Mission Calamajué

FOREWORD

WALLACE STEGNER was the first man to speak of wilderness as part of the geography of hope. The paragraphs leading to his hope appear on the facing page and are part of a letter Professor Stegner wrote to Mr. David Pesonen for the Outdoor Recreation Resources Review Commission. In 1961 Secretary of the Interior Stewart L. Udall threw away a speech he had prepared and read the letter instead. We endorse it, and have been borrowing lines from it ever since.

The wilderness we have to hope about consists of islands, not too well marked on any map, and not understood well enough yet. Pending that understanding, there should be some sort of protectorate set up for them in men's hearts, if not their laws. Let them be cared for, under the eye of the International Union for Conservation, by poets, practical men, and others—all others —who will not get along very well if we ever let these islands disappear.

Baja California is one island of hope; this book suggests that there are several, and is an introduction to their geography. It is a geography we can all hope to inquire into, on the ground and at our leisure, one of these days. We fully expect to get there, and to get to a good many other places on this civilized planet that a good technology is making so small and easy to reach the wild edge of. I hope that bad technology will not have wiped wildness out before I make it. More important, I hope that it won't be wiped out before my children get there, and their grandchildren.

These places don't need to go. They do not have to be an arena in which man carries on his old habits and makes his old mistakes until the naturalness of a place is demolished or even demeaned. Man's genius, if he really has one, can surely find ways to go back over the bruised places, heal them, and let them sustain his civilization. There isn't enough unspoiled land left to sustain his old habits. Old habits could wipe it out in a decade or two; four at most. But that unspoiled land, that wilderness, wherein the evolutionary force that put man on this planet still succeeds, can add meaning to his civilization as long as wilderness and civilization last. Wilderness can, that is, if man lets it.

Baja California has places where man can let wilderness last if he elects to. They will help us to remember that man can never put the wilderness back. It doesn't work that way. Baja is a good place to respect what man discovers there and leaves alone, not what he brings there to change it, wherever he comes from. It is a place to learn. Without Baja's wildness, the world is just that much closer to becoming a cage.

The Sierra Club plainly has territorial ambitions. It got them from a Scotsman who, by way of Wisconsin, walked a thousand miles to a Gulf, explored an expanse of ice that was named Muir Glacier in his honor, knew the Sierra Nevada well enough to call it the Range of Light, furthered the national park idea, fathered the Sierra Club, and died, probably of grief, when the world lost a Yosemite. In the course of his first summer in the Sierra—when he was thirty—he noted in his journal that "when we try to pick out anything by itself, we find it hitched to everything else in the universe." The club he founded is making the same observation. Organizations working in behalf of the wilderness idea are learning that interest in the work is universal. People who share the interest are getting a new idea about who the have-not nations are. We need aid from people who have lived at peace with their land far longer than we. And we suspect that the use of bulldozers and pesticides we send abroad to aid foreign places should be overseen by native ecologists.

We by no means have all the answers yet, but we are learning from Joseph Wood Krutch and his good-humored appreciation not only of Baja California and other places, but also of pertinent human frailties and potentials. No desert ever had a better friend than he, unless it is Eliot Porter. Wild places of the earth that have not been described by their respective pen and lens are unfortunate. Both are working as fast as they can to help explain these places. Dr. Porter is in the Grand Canyon, for the second time in a summer, as this book goes to press. The Brooks Range, Kenya, Cape Horn, the Great Smokies, and Nebraska are on his agenda, as well as the warbler or two he has not yet photographed. If Dr. Krutch will let us, we will use his words often in the blending of words and photographs we have in mind about the miracle that the life stream is, and that man should diminish no longer.

If Sierra Club books do as much for wilderness in the United States as many a kind, eminent man has said they have done, then it is time for us to travel afield in search of our subjects. Wilderness is becoming one of the endangered species of environment on the planet Earth. In it is an essential that man could run out of even before he loses breathable air and rational judgment. Man has been busying himself, in the brief flash of two centuries of technological revolution, with wiping out the organic variety the world has been made of. He has learned how to root it out, but has not worried very much about whether the eradication is a good idea.

We think man should worry. Wilderness has produced on this planet a variety of living things that primitive people had the sense to wonder at. This organic variety is inseparable from the natural beauty that civilized man is forgetting how to see. The wilderness that is home to uncounted varieties of life belongs to all those varieties, they belong to it, and man in all his colors is only one of them. As long as wilderness endures, it will be the continuum from which new beauty can come forth, part of the natural succession that preceded man by billions of years and can be expected to survive him, however badly he impairs it before he leaves. In Wildness is the preservation of the World, and of man.

DAVID BROWER
Executive Director, Sierra Club

San Francisco
September 20, 1967

CONTENTS

SEVENTY-THREE COLOR PLATES

INTRODUCTION

"**B**AJA CALIFORNIA is a wonderful example of how much bad roads can do for a country." This observation is cribbed from something I wrote after one of my early visits to that long, lonely, and beautiful peninsula. In addition to being the simple truth, it embodies a warning.

Nature gave to Baja nearly all of the beauties possible in a dry, warm climate—towering mountains, flowery desert flats, blue water, bird-rich islands, and scores of great, curving beaches as fine as the best anywhere in the world. All of this has remained very nearly inviolate just because very little of what we call progress has marred it. Baja has never needed protection because the land protected itself.

Nearly a hundred years before the Pilgrims arrived in New England, one of Cortez's captains landed not far from what is now the capital city of La Paz. But it was more than 150 years later, and after a number of failures, that the first permanent mission settlement was founded. Presently others were built and for a time they flourished. Then came a decline, and by the beginning of the nineteenth century even the missionaries had given up. The peninsula was returned to its own keeping.

The principal reason for this fortunate situation was not, of course, any appreciation for natural beauty, much less any desire to protect it. Primarily, it was simply because the land offered so little of what men then desired. One of the eighteenth century padres assessed it thus:

"Everything concerning California is of such little importance that it is hardly worth the trouble to take a pen and write about it. Of poor shrubs, useless thorn bushes and bare rocks, of miles of sand without water or woods, of a handful of people who, beside their physical shape and ability to think, have nothing to distinguish them from animals, what shall I or what can I report?"

In the next century Lieutenant Ives, the first citizen of the United States to see Grand Canyon, described the canyon in much the same spirit: "Ours has been the first and will doubtless be the last party of whites to visit this profitless locality. It seems intended by nature that the Colorado River, along the greater portion of its lonely and majestic way, shall be forever unvisited and undisturbed." Too much wild beauty was nearly everywhere available to be much valued for its own sake. It was to be a long time before we began to realize that beauty of that kind was becoming increasingly scarce in a society glibly described as "abundant."

In 1848, a happy chance saved Baja California for the second time: the peninsula was not annexed by the United States. Those charged with negotiating the peace treaty with Mexico were instructed to ask for it but not to insist too strongly if giving it up appeared to have bargaining value as an apparent concession. Mexico did want to keep it, and thanks to that, the peninsula has remained even today almost as unscarred as it ever was. Had we been a little more insistent or Mexico's attitude a little more yielding, there is no doubt what would have happened. Baja certainly would have been opened up for tourism and "recreation." The finest of the unspoiled beaches would certainly have become before now what the Southern California beaches are—recreation areas valuable in their way but offering no more than a sorry, vestigial remnant of any real contact with what unspoiled natural beauty has to offer. Good roads would have been built and it is easy to see what that would have meant. The peninsula is about 800 miles long. Today a blacktop road runs the 128 miles from the border town of Mexicali to what was once the remote fishing village of San Felipe on the Gulf of California side of the peninsula. The result of this present road is a weekend flow of thousands crowding the narrow streets, patronizing the noisy taverns and creating in San Felipe the atmosphere of a Mexican border town, a minor Tijuana or Nogales. Not one out of a hundred Anglo invaders drives his car so much as a hundred yards past the blacktop, but if the road were extended at least half of them would follow it to the end. There are many people who want (or think they want) silence, solitude, and unspoiled nature just enough to push into and destroy all three. They will push as far as, but no farther than, good roads will take them.

Bad roads act as filters. They separate those who are sufficiently appreciative of what lies beyond the blacktop to be willing to undergo mild inconvenience from that much larger number of travelers which is not willing. The rougher the road, the finer the filter. Today any traveler who undertakes to drive a four-wheeled vehicle the length of the peninsula from border to cape will discover, not so very far below San Felipe, that the filter becomes very fine indeed.

The moral of this discussion of bad roads is not what the advocates of maximum accessibility and unlimited development try to saddle the rest of us with. It is not that "the people" should be kept out of the areas which are properly theirs and that these areas should be reserved for a privileged few who happen to have rather unusual tastes. No one in his right mind objects to recreational areas and maximum accessibility for them. The moral is simply this: development of recreational facilities and the presence of large crowds transforms any natural area into something quite artificial. Despite all the talk about multiple use, some uses are incompatible with others. Quiet contemplation cannot be practiced on the borders of a lake full of speed boats and water skiers. We must either accept as inevitable a near future in which contact with unspoiled nature has become impossible nearly everywhere within the boundaries of our country or, on the other hand, recognize the distinction between those remaining natural areas which should, and those which should not, be developed. A generation ago Aldo Leopold was one of the first to recognize the impasse which was being approached when he wrote:

"Recreation became a problem with a name in the days of the elder Roosevelt . . . when the railroads which had banished the countryside from the city began to carry city dwellers en masse to the countryside. . . . The automobile has spread this once mild and local predicament to the outermost limits of good roads. . . . The weekenders radiate from every town, generating heat and friction as they go. . . . Bureaus build roads into new hinterlands, then buy more hinterlands to absorb the exodus accelerated by the roads. . . . To him who seeks in the woods and mountains only those things obtainable from travel or golf, the present situation is tolerable. But to him who seeks something more, recreation has become a self-destructive process of seeking but never quite finding, a major frustration of mechanized society."

It is probably true that more people prefer recreation areas than prefer areas that remain as nature made them. But the recognition of minority rights is no more undemocratic when those rights have to do with tastes and esthetic preferences than it is when they involve political opinions. In Baja the minority can be joined by anyone willing to pay the very small price required to enter areas not served by good roads.

When roads are too good, too wide, and too fast, they not only become eyesores themselves but are, at the same time, invitations to those who have no real interest in what they lead to. Nor is it always popular demand which is responsible for their construction. Road builders, dam builders, and predator poisoners constitute a special interest group with a voice they should not have in national affairs. It is to their advantage to keep busy. Too often they build roads or dams for which there is neither real need nor real demand.

A few years ago General Motors sponsored a television short intended to make driving less hazardous. One of the bits of advice volunteered by the narrator as the screen showed a motorist speeding along a superhighway was "Forget the scenery!" This injunction soon disappeared from the screen, perhaps because someone called the sponsor's attention to that favorite argument of the road builders: Roads, they say, not only enhance scenic beauty, they also make more of it accessible to the motorist who is enabled to contemplate more miles of it while driving at 80 mph.

How long will it be before the twentieth century catches up with Baja California? In ways that affect only an insignificant portion of Baja's area, it has already begun do to so. Every year a few more adventurous visitors drive cars (preferably with four-wheeled drive) along its often atrocious roads, roads which meander from one tiny village or one-family ranch to the next, along trails sketched out more than a century ago by the burros carrying Spanish padres from mission to mission. Private planes, which can land on a few paved strips near commercially operated motels or on any one of quite a number of just usable clearings near a village, bring a considerably larger number—most of whom, alas, are less interested in scenic beauty than in slaughtering the disappearing wild fauna or fishing for marlin (the latter an enterprise which sometimes suggests Oscar Wilde's description of a fox hunt: "the unspeakable in pursuit of the inedible.") In a land where game wardens hardly exist, the so-called sportsmen are threatening the osprey, for example, with extinction in accordance with that inner injunction of many hunters: "If it moves, shoot it!"

Besides modest accommodations for fishermen and the occasional traveler by automobile, there are three luxury hotels (two of them very recent) which have been built at the southern-most cape, though they as yet are reachable only by private plane or over still-bad roads. That leaves a lot of Baja California in another century—almost 800 miles of it, very nearly untouched, from San Felipe to La Paz and from La Paz to the cape. There is, indeed, many a square mile in the mountains, far from even the sketchy highways and visited only by a few villagers living in isolated villages, or not visited at all.

Most of Baja California lies within the boundaries of the Sonoran Desert, and its scenery has important affinities with Southern Arizona, much of which is part of the same desert. The region lies south of the Arizona desert, however, and in addition to the many Arizona plants there are others unknown outside Baja California. There are also certain species closely related to those of the Arizona flora but with a tropical brilliance. The flaming red mistletoe or the almost equally vivid Fairy Duster make related Arizona species seem tame in comparison. It is the combination of the familiar and the strange which makes the region so unusually attractive to those for whom the desert has a special fascination.

The strange is very strange, even to a man from Arizona. The giant cardon cactus takes the place of the Arizona saguaro; the grotesque elephant tree with its tapering and contorted branches attracts the attention of the least observant traveler, as does the boogum tree. Off the west coast schools of gray whales make their annual pilgrimage to their breeding grounds in Scammon's Lagoon, and they sometimes round the cape to sail up into the Sea of Cortez. In the bluest of skies the man-of-war bird opens or closes its long twin tail feathers; long lines of pelicans sail majestically by; and blue or brown-footed boobies plummet from high headfirst into the sea.

The chances are that large areas of Baja will remain for a long time unspoiled, but even so, the Mexican government may soon have to decide (as our government still has not decided) whether it is worthwhile to call a halt to certain kinds of exploitation which already threaten the things which, once lost, can never be recovered. An American company evaporating salt on a very large scale near Scammon's Lagoon is proposing to deepen the shallow water where the gray whales breed and may bring about the extinction of a spectacular species, a species once believed destroyed by whalers but now making a fine recovery just where the salt company wants more salt. Until a year or two ago there was, I think, no wildlife refuge in all Mexico. Now a beginning has been made with the sanctuary on Baza Island where commercial egg collectors threatened to destroy two species, the elegant tern and Heermann's gull, birds which breed there and, except for a few individuals, nowhere else. More recently still, the government has begun to discuss the possibility of making Tiburon Island near the mainland a game preserve. Hopefully the government will continue this trend, and will take over when Baja California's roads cease to be bad enough.

*　　*　　*

Eliot Porter's photographs, for all their detail and realism, are not just a traveler's record of Baja, they are works of art which record an individual artist's special vision. Looked at from one point of view, they are primarily mood and pattern pictures. In this respect they belong in the finest tradition of modern art. But they are fundamentally different from pure abstractions because the moods are generated by external nature and the patterns are those discovered in nature, not purely human inventions. Porter's is an art which reasserts the old conviction that nature is the source of all beauty and the sole inspiration of art. Much of modern painting turns its back on nature and attempts to affirm man's independence of her. These photographs, on the other hand, reaffirm the conviction of those among us who hold firm to the belief that "in wildness is the preservation of the world," not merely because wildness is a source of health and joy but also because it supplies at least the hint seized upon and emphasized by even the least representational forms of art when they are at their best.

The tendency of avant garde painting is to express, and often proclaim, what it is now fashionable to call man's alienation from the universe outside himself, from its external forms which no longer interest him and from its laws or its lawlessness which correspond in no way to his human values or needs. He must, some say today, create his own forms in the graphic or plastic arts just as he must create his own esthetics and ethics because nature supplies no hint of either. This constitutes what the existentialist calls his freedom but it also makes inevitable that alienation which he often admits to be almost intolerably bleak.

The "nature lover" and conservationist—even if he happens to be one of those to whom the visual arts make little appeal—has more of a stake than he realizes in this conflict between the alienated art now so much in favor and that of the artist who, like Porter, finds his inspiration in nature and feels himself not alienated from, but very much a part of her. The sense that nature is the most beautiful of all spectacles and something of which man is a part; that she is a source of health and joy which inevitably dries up when man is alienated from her; these are the ultimate reasons why it seems to us desperately important that the works of nature should not disappear to be replaced by the works of man alone.

Joseph Wood Krutch

Tuscon, Arizona
February 19, 1967

WILD PENINSULA

M Y INTEREST in deserts came about through my reading *The Twelve Seasons*, a beautiful
little book about Connecticut country, not deserts, written by Joseph Wood Krutch.
It led to an association with Krutch in my book on Thoreau and to the discovery of
his *Desert Year* and *Voice of the Desert*. I learned about his journeys into Baja California by plane and
truck, about a wild, inaccessible, and almost-forgotten peninsula, about vegetation adapted to
the austere climate, about hidden springs high on bare brown mountains, and blue coves with
sandy beaches tucked away along the shore. I determined to see it myself.

My first trip to Baja was to be a dry run for an expedition to another desert country, the
Galápagos Islands. I did not guess that out of this trial expedition the desire would arise to see
more of the peninsula at another time of year. I did not think I would ever do a book on it.

The first expedition began in winter with cold nights and windy days. We entered the peninsula on the very arid gulf coast side where the sparse plant life was still dormant. When we
returned by the humid Pacific route two and a half months later, the more varied and denser
vegetation of the Pacific side, in response to the moisture of ocean fogs, was beginning to come
to life. We were by then in a hurry to get home and didn't stop often to photograph. I knew I was
neglecting opportunities and began at that time to think about coming back.

My return to Lower California, in July and August of 1966, lasted only a month, but was in
many ways a much more productive trip than the first. I had a specific goal in mind—a book
on Baja.

July and August are the time of the summer rains, if there are to be any, and many of the
plants might be blooming. I was warned that it would be hot, and indeed it was, but not uni-
formly hot. The weather varied greatly across the peninsula, from warm summer temperatures
on the Pacific side to oppressive heat on the Gulf. The difference was the Pacific Ocean and its
cool on-shore breezes. We swam off Pacific beaches in water at a comfortable temperature of
75° Fahrenheit, with air at less than 90°. On the Gulf the water was like a hot bath and not very
refreshing; you could lie in it and feel no cooler than on the beach. The real difference was in
the heat on land, an enervating weight you carried around with you all the time, slowing your
steps and requiring a great investment of energy to overcome. When all the truck cab venti-
lators were wide open, our slow speed created a breeze that brought respite, but when we
stopped and stepped out, the sun's heat was like the blast from a hot-air dryer. I had to be more
than passingly motivated to stand up against it, and many times questioned whether the photograph was worth the effort.

To avoid the hundred miles of paved roads down either coast we chose a central route through
the Sierra Juarez, a mile high plateau of pines and aspen forest—cool country. Summer thunder-

storms rumbled around in the afternoons and the sandy road was filled with puddles. As we worked our way south to lower altitudes we left the pines behind but not the thunderstorms. The landscape changed to brown rolling hills thickly covered with a brushy chaparral. The low shrubs and plants had passed their flowering peak and were dropping petals from withered rusty heads. The aspect was that of autumn. Even the leaves of the plants had lost their high green and had faded to a yellow-olive. The sandy ground was strewn with dried bits and pieces of the brittle vegetation, a clear indication that the fruiting season in this part of Baja was drawing to a close despite the persistence of rainstorms.

The network of roads that threaded the high country gave out about a hundred miles below the border at Valle Trinidad, and from there a fairly well-traveled road went east to San Felipe on the Gulf, and a little-traveled, badly washed-out road led to the Pacific coastal highway below Ensenada. We took the road less traveled. It was rocky and narrow and led over a series of progressively lower ridges through wild uninhabited country. The grades were steep even for our jeeps. The road circled mountain shoulders, dropped abruptly into tight ravines, sloped across hillsides at a slant—never wide and sometimes barely the width of our trucks, a road just scratched on the surface to remove the boulders, badly gullied and eroded, leading always downward from one rise to the next lower one. In some places an outcrop of rock was all that had saved the road from obliteration; in others the road had been cut into so deeply that the outside wheels of our trucks bounced across the gap.

Everywhere were quail; the country was full of them. We constantly flushed fat coveys and family groups from the sides of the road. Often they would run ahead of us in seeming panic, unable to decide on which rise to seek cover and reluctant to take wing. We saw two kinds, the topknotted California quail and the scaled quail named for its scale-like feather pattern. Almost anywhere we stopped and turned off our motor we could hear their conversational clucking and muttering as they foraged in the underbrush.

Turning inland at El Rosario we saw our first boogums, *Idria columnaris,* called cirios by the Mexicans because of the resemblance to the wax tapers used in their churches. The trunk tapers rapidly toward the top, where it ends in a tuft of nondescript short branches; it is widest near the ground but often restricted at ground level, giving the tree a precariously balanced appearance. The branches are short, tangled, and stiff, growing sparse, disheveled, and with no detectible plan. If there is enough rain to encourage them, they put forth small spatulate leaves like those of their relative, the ocotillo. In time of drought, which is the prevailing time, the leaves are promptly abandoned to conserve moisture. As in many of the xerophilous families, photosynthesis relies the year around upon the green stems and bark. The cirio has persistent thorns that are modifications of its leaves. Some of the trunks branch high up into double or triple tops; some branch low, looping down to the ground or bending out to the side and curving up again like waving independent tentacles. In the blooming season the end of each of these arms bears a spray of flowers, small, sweet-smelling, pale-yellow blossoms in clusters at the ends of stalks that fan out like sparklers on the Fourth of July.

Farther east and south, in the higher country, the common barrel cactus was putting out orange-yellow buds and flowers from the cluster of orange fish-hook spines at its top, the flowers scarcely distinguishable from the spines. *Lophocereus Schottii,* a columnar cactus with thick mats of down-drooping, gray spines at the ends of its columns, was sporting pink blossoms along the vertical rows of its ribs. The machaerocereus, a sprawling, branching cactus extremely common on the peninsula (its sap is used as fish poison) was also in flower—long pink and white funnels with flaring petals that we saw only in the early morning; later in the day they were always closed and wilted.

At El Mármol we saw the first elephant trees in bloom. I never would have guessed, having seen them in winter, that elephant trees could put on such a show of feathery pink fluorescence. At a distance they looked like peach trees in full bloom. Looking closely we saw every twig covered with clusters of tiny flowers, each with a faint perfume. Like the cirios, they had cast their leaves aside to save water, and were now staking all on producing their seeds, the durable packages that would outlast any drought. Like arctic and desert annuals, and like some people, they were rushing production to assure survival until the next favorable opportunity for growth.

Near Santa Catarina Landing, in hilly country where the elephant tree was predominant, we discovered that the blossoms are not always pink; some are yellow and others salmon colored. In the late afternoon light, with ridge behind ridge of misty hills fading into the distant Pacific haze, the landscape was like a fairyland, a setting for an operatic fantasy, and it was hard to believe that the pink and yellow trees were real. I half expected to see trolls in peaked hats with picks and shovels on their shoulders march across the stage or a ballerina appear suddenly from the wings. The scene could as easily have been a vista in a Chinese painting. The gnarled and distorted trees with their backlit, exaggerated burden of blossoms seemed a substitute for a more complicated and common reality; the distant planes of hills in filmy aerial perspective seemed a disguise that concealed the true substance and solidity of a harsher land.

At Santa Catarina Landing, where the onyx mined at El Mármol was once shipped out to Ensenada and San Diego, all traces of the loading docks and ramps have disappeared. We could see why. The Pacific waves were breaking in never-ceasing sequence on the hard gray sand. Out beyond the shelving beach, in blue deep water, incipient waves appeared one by one, increasing in size as they raced toward land. Nearing it, and top-heavy, they fell forward and disintegrated into foam. They lost speed but continued their rush up the sloping sand, to lose their energy at last in a thin sheet of water bordered with bubbles and bits of things from the sea. Each wave was following an order about what waves must do that antedated the planet, and yet each wave did this its own unique way, bringing gifts that had never been seen before. There was a scatter of kelp and seaweed, but the long, wide beach gave the impression of spotless purity—and the assurance that absolute purity would be restored in good time. Little evidence of occupation by man remained; the debris of his activities had been swept away. But behind the line of dunes above the beach, dragged there for salvage, the rusting shell of a lifeboat bore on its stern the name *Boxer*, and on a low stony hill overlooking the dunes a group of weathered wooden crosses, a sagging fence, and heaps of rough volcanic stones outlined a graveyard, neglected how long we could not tell.

*   *   *

Never go to Baja California once; go at least twice. The first trip will be a journey into the unknown. Every village, every settlement, every ranch, and every crossroad the first time will be new and unforeseen. Every turn in the road and every hill may be an adventure. However, it may be just enough adventure to keep anxiety high and assurance low. The second time reverses the situation. You almost know what to expect, how steep the grades and rocky the roads will be, what kind of repairs to anticipate. You know about cactus spines and their insidious way of working through the tread to puncture the tube and break off, and you know how to find and extract them so that they can cause no trouble later.

For all the anxiety in it, I liked especially what the first trip revealed to us when we crossed the peninsula at its narrowest point to Miller's Landing, long since abandoned, and camped amid large pearly sea snails, then went south to Scammon's Lagoon. We felt some of the joy of discovery that Captain Scammon must have felt on finding it. He kept its location secret for years while he reaped a fortune in oil. When the secret was finally uncovered by other ship captains, the whales were brought close to extinction by profligate slaughter of both adults and calves, until at last they were afforded international protection. The gray whales are making a recovery; after years of absence, they have returned to their ancestral breeding place in these warm shallow waters. Here once more they bear, nurse, and protect their young during the first few weeks of their lives.

At Guerrero Negro, the company town of the large salt works on the northern shore of Black Warrior Lagoon, we drove along the dykes of the salt pans to the shore of an arm of Scammon's Lagoon from which we could see the whales. They were just beginning to arrive from the arctic waters of the Bering Sea; pregnant cows, yearlings, and adults that had come to breed. We could see the whales out on the shimmering water near the horizon as they rose to breathe or leapt clear of the surface, their bodies a mirage above the glassy water of the lagoon. Like opaque bubbles they swelled out of the undefined confluence of sky and water, were tenuously attached for a moment, then separated themselves and for a moment became floating balloons on the horizon.

At night the whales came in closer to shore and we could hear their blowing more clearly. Their prolonged sighing inspirations sounded primordial—a false impression, for cetaceans are new to this world. For me it was a restless night. Through the long moonlit hours I lay stimulated and wakeful, listening to the slow rhythm of their powerful breathing, interrupted occasionally by a slap and a splash. These were the sounds of the world from which most men had excluded themselves. Lying there, unexcluded, I imagined that I was on some long-vanished Mesozoic shore and that any moment a fearsome, pachydermatous reptile would come lumbering over the mud flats out of the lagoon.

*　　*　　*

Most of Baja California is included by Edmund C. Jaeger in the Sonoran Desert, which he classified in six divisions. The central part of the peninsula from El Rosario on the Pacific south to the latitude of La Paz, with the exception of a narrow strip along the Gulf of California, he calls the Viscaíno-Magdalena Desert. The coastal strip he divided at Bahía de Los Angeles between the northern Colorado Desert and the southern Gulf Coast Desert, which extends to the tip of the peninsula. Both these strips are subdivisions of the Sonoran Desert.

Dryness, it will surprise no one to learn, is the principal characteristic of deserts; but how dry must a desert be? Geographers generally agree that areas that receive less than ten inches of unevenly distributed rain a year and have a relatively high mean annual temperature are desert. There are undoubtedly hotter places in North America than the Viscaíno Desert, but it would be hard to find any that are drier. In some parts of the Viscaíno Desert we learned that no rain had fallen for six years; ranches were being abandoned as wells dried. In other parts the road proved that rain had fallen not too long ago. Wherever the road crossed wide arroyos or dry lake beds, we were slowed to a crawl by deep ruts and potholes, dug by trucks when the ground was wet. To avoid being mired in the ruts of previous vehicles, each successive driver had attempted to find other routes through the worst places and had made a vast network of tracks, acres in extent, all equally bad. It was easy to see how the rain made enormous miles-wide seas of mud. The rains must have been torrential, if short-lived, filling arroyos to the brim, over-flowing the level lands, converting the silt of other storms into a sticky, slippery, impassable morass. We heard of cloudbursts that made the roads unusable for months.

Eventually the ground dries out and it is possible to get through again, but the ruts and holes remain and are deepened by the traffic. The soil is pulverized by passing wheels and slides into hollows, filling them with brown powder. One does not become bogged down in these dust bins; instead the dust is thrown out in billowing clouds that envelop the vehicle, hiding it completely from view. Often all one can see of a car ahead is a moving plume of brown smoke that seems to erupt from the earth.

When a car plunges into a dust pocket, a cloud squirts up on all sides. If the car is open the driver and passengers choke, their eyes smart, and they see nothing until they stop and wait for the dust to settle. In a closed car things are not so bad, but the powder sifts in through every crack and is never pleasant. A brown precipitate slides down the windows in rivulets. To see out even to the front of his own car, the driver must turn on the windshield wiper. Then you come out of the tunnel into daylight, to discover a jaundiced complexion. Your hair is powdered with the same makeup that clings to your eyebrows and eyelashes and that clogs your nose. The dust covers your clothing and skin and wherever there was sweat there are streaks of mud. Only your eyes remain uncoated, and they peer out, holes in the mask.

The paradox of the Viscaíno Desert, especially near the Pacific coast, is that the trees and shrubs, and even some of the larger forms of cactus, are festooned with moisture-loving epi-phytes that depend upon their hosts for support. Parasites grow there too—mistletoes and a species without chlorophyll called "witches' hair" that completely envelops elephant trees in a web of yellow filaments. Many of the epiphytes are flowering plants belonging to the bromiliad family. They are particularly noticeable on the ocotillo, but also grow on palo verde and the other thorny leguminous trees. There is also a variety of olive-green lichen, quite similar to the beard moss of the northern coniferous forests, that hangs in trailing strands from all the vegetation, and does so most luxuriously near the coast. The moisture that sustains them comes from ocean fogs that roll in over the land at night and lie during the early hours of the day in misty layers among the hills until the rising sun disperses them. These plants are unknown on the hotter, drier gulf side of the peninsula, where fog does not occur.

For all its general aridity, Baja California contains many inhabited oases on its mountainous spine. Some are small, one-family settlements like the green pocket at Santa Catarina, half way from El Mármol to the landing, or like Arroyo Catavina, noted for its blue palms. Others are big enough to support villages of several hundred people; San Ignacio is the most famous of these. All the large oases receive their water from springs or streams. San Ignacio's wide canyon contains prolific springs that provide water for irrigation. San Miguel de Comondú and San José de Comondú, two communities farther south, also depend on spring water. Like San Ig-nacio, they are situated in a canyon eroded into a massive lava flow, and the sides of the canyon culminate in vertical walls of columnar basalt. Along the floor of the canyon crystal-clear, channelled streams flow perpetually and water a luxuriant wild vegetation as well as fields culti-vated in the rich volcanic soil. Stream-nourished oases like Mulegé are situated on permanent rivers that are small trickles in times of drought but are destructive torrents during summer cloudbursts. Most of the family ranches along the peninsula are not natural oases; they have no surface water and depend on wells for livestock and small truck gardens.

Bahía de La Concepción, nearly landlocked and twenty-five miles long, is one of the most beautiful places on the gulf coast north of La Paz. Turquoise and ultramarine waters wash its precipitous shores with the milky blueness of tropical seas the world over. The color, produced by colloidal limes derived from the shells and skeletons of myriad marine animals, is the same as the color produced by colloidal suspensions in glacial streams and travertine springs. Arcs of shell-sand beaches gleam at the ends of sheltered coves; mangrove thickets occupy the muddy shallows; ribbons of pale green seaweed wash from the rocks at low tide and come to rest in windrows at the edge of the waves. Mountains almost surround the bay. At one end the land slants gently up to a low pass and is covered with a forest of giant cardon cactus; it is the densest stand I have seen in Baja California, many of the trees being more than fifty feet tall. The boulder-strewn slopes are clad sparsely in a desert growth of thorny shrubs, tangled ocotillo, and ghostly, white-barked palo blanco trees. Beautiful as the vegetation is, it does not invite carefree exploration as do temperate deciduous woodlands; it is armed against intrusion. But its hostility shrinks with distance; details blend into the uniformity of the mass, and as one moves still farther away, the mountainsides display their ancient volcanic beginnings, their sedimentary layers and cliffs of basalt, a tapestry in rock that fades to thin pastels on the ranges across the bay. There is a contradiction; the harshness of the known immediate environment denies the agreeableness of the remote and unverifiable scene, denies its dreamlike unreality, and the feeling that one experience is truer than the other sets up a counterpoint that arouses a bewildered exaltation.

Baja California is epitomized by this resplendent bay, where the real and the romantic are juxtaposed, just as other opposites are up and down the lower and wilder California—the chill winds against the oppressive heat; torrents and mud against the dusty desiccation; forested shade against desert waste. The vegetation itself seems to defy the seasons. Leaves are born in winter and blossoms in summer. Fall, the season of ripening, may come in spring; and spring may come if it rains. The bare, leafless bones of the elephant trees stand against the lava chunks and gravel. In the heat of mid-July they bring forth fluffy masses of the most delicate, fragrant flowers. The very geology testifies to agony on a grand scale, when the granite spine and its metamorphic core, upheaved in eons past, was shattered by volcanic thrusts and buried in the ensuing floods of lava.

What has saved Baja California up to the present from the fate that has overtaken most of California and almost all the Pacific coast of the United States and Mexico is, as Dr. Krutch has said, the state of its roads. They are primitive to say the least. Under the best of conditions following long periods of drought they are passable by four-wheel-drive vehicles, most trucks, and passenger cars with high clearance. Low-slung modern automobiles would be hung up in the rougher places and their gas tanks and oil pans would be punctured by rocks. By the judicious selection of routes some might get through to La Paz, but the trip would be an ordeal and they would surely sustain considerable damage. Following heavy rain, the occurrence of which is as unpredictable as is its intensity, the roads become a morass of mud where they cross arroyos and outwash plains, and are impassable to all vehicles but hovercraft, and I'm not sure about them.

Roads in Baja are natural developments, like boogum trees or Mexican graveyards. The roads there were not planned by engineers in anticipation of future population densities and traffic flows. They were not planned at all, but grew as the people needed them, no faster than people needed them. The Highway Commission is not as ambitious or as sovereign in lower California as it is in upper. The Mexican government spent almost nothing on construction of Baja's roads and spends a similar amount on keeping them up. Many of Baja's roads were built by miners to get their ore to the nearest port. Mines closed but the roads remained, and the operators of later mines farther up or down the peninsula connected their new roads with the old—sensibly, to avoid having to find new ports on the coast near them. In this way Baja's road system grew, and now will take you the length of the peninsula.

The Baja road is just a narrow track in the desert, often invisible in clouds of dust, sometimes not there at all after a good storm; but it is the center of life in the Central Desert and most of the rest of Baja. All human commerce moves along it, and has always moved, within the memory of the peninsula's longest inhabitants. It is a part of the spirit of the land in a way that no six or eight lane creation of highway engineering can be.

The helpful state of the roads is a fortunate corollary to an accident of history by which President Polk failed to include Baja California in the land ceded to the United States following the war with Mexico. If it had been ceded, we can safely assume that modern highways would now have simplified the irregular mountainous coastline on both sides of the peninsula, and would be delivering an endless stream of automobile traffic to beach and cove and bay from San Diego and the mouth of the Colorado River to Cabo San Lucas, eight hundred fifty miles to the south. Human preëmption of the land, something presently associated with progress, has already begun; the advance of a kind of civilization can be seen in the developments taking place along both coasts. For one hundred miles south of the border to San Felipe on the Gulf and almost to El Rosario on the Pacific, the works of man are spreading from foci of inoculation like the growth of mold in bread. How the growth takes place is not our business—unless it is the Americans north of the border who are insinuating spores of the mold upon the Americans south of the Border.

Luckily, a trend in the technology of transportation is slowing down the overland advance, a pincers movement dependent on the automobile, and moving fast in many places. The new trend is the development of private flying and small commercial air operations, which accommodate a hurried industrial civilization in which people are becoming increasingly impatient in their work and in their recreation. Everything must be done in a hurry and less intensely; and paradoxically as more time becomes available for going, less time seems available for seeing. The destination becomes the goal and the route hardly matters. Thus the airplane replaces the automobile, and remote places need no longer aggravate man's acquired impatience. Whether or not this is good for the traveler, it is good for the land. The pressure applied by motorists for better roads has relaxed; the ordinary incentive of industrial need does not exist in Baja California, so the roads remain unimproved.

In several hours, instead of days or weeks, vacationists are able to reach their destinations along the coastline of Baja California. They can fly to Bahía de San Quintín, to Bahía San Louis Gonzaga, to Bahía de Los Angeles, to Mulegé, to Loreto, to La Paz, and to Cabo San Lucas, all places where landing strips have been cleared for small planes (and La Paz can handle jets). At the bays fishing boats are available and accommodations of ever increasing luxuriousness are being provided. What to many travelers are barren mountain ranges and desert plains of little interest, and hot, dry, and dusty too, can be avoided easily. The adventurous and curious can still make the long, slow, often uncomfortable, but always fascinating journey by truck to these places. The road people will not provide much economic support for the resort. They may pause briefly for a night or two to diminish the accumulated dust, hunger, and need for rest—

until a restlessness for the rutted winding road and ever-unfolding landscape calls them back once more to the hostile interior, where uncertainty is the stimulus and adventure is the reward.

Visitors to Baja California will certainly continue to increase in number, but most of them will go to the coastal oases for short vacations, weekend fishing, perhaps here and there for golf. In a hurry to make the most of limited time, they will fly and they will be well taken care of. When they return home they will tell their friends about the comforts of the places they have visited, and the next year their friends will go too, and these oases will thrive.

But the vast areas of the peninsula in between can remain vacant. To them will come a slow trickle of motorists in jeeps and trucks, not to stay but to pass through. The adventure of the journey, the wonder of the topography and of all the strange and unusual living things—these will preoccupy. By the accepted definition of roadlessness most of Baja is wilderness, explorable only on foot or on horse. Transected, however, by unimproved roads it still offers a kind of experience, rapidly becoming unattainable in developed places, that of exploration by motor. In my youth, in 1922, I sought and found adventure by driving west in a Model T Ford on roads no less primitive than those that exist today in Baja California.

Perhaps in Baja the resources for these two kinds of recreation can be divisibly maintained: on the one hand well-planned coastal oases for those who need them and value their settings; on the other a wild interior respected and saved for its very wildness.

The wildness can remain part of the beyond, part of what can always add meaning and uniqueness to the oases themselves, part of what is elsewhere going too fast, part of every man's geography of hope.

ELIOT PORTER

ACKNOWLEDGEMENTS. I wish to thank all those who made my two trips into Baja California possible. On the first expedition in 1964 from February into April we traveled in three vehicles: two universal Jeeps and a Jeep pickup with camper. My son Stephen was indispensable as both driver and mechanic; his wife Kathy took charge of the commissary and cooking. Tom Mayer acted as interpreter and shared driving of one of the Jeeps with David MacIntosh. In July and August 1966, with two vehicles, we drove only half the length of the peninsula. Steve's older brother Jonathan and his wife Zoe kept the expedition going. Bob Judson gave invaluable assistance as a driver and through his fluency in Spanish.

E. P.

1. To Have Known the Desert

Los huesos son relámpagos
en la noche del cuerpo.
Oh mundo, todo es noche
y la vida es relámpago.

Our bones are lightning
in the night of the flesh.
O world, all is night,
life is the lightning.

It is not easy to live in that continuous awareness of things which alone
is true living. Even those who make a parade of their conviction that sunset,
rain, and the growth of a seed are daily miracles are not usually so
much impressed by them as they urge others to be. The faculty of wonder
tires easily and a miracle which happens everyday is a miracle no longer,
no matter how many times one tells oneself that it ought to be.
Life would seem a great deal longer and a great deal fuller than it does if it
were not for the fact that the human being is, by nature, a creature to whom
"O altitudo" is much less natural than "So what!" Really to see
something once or twice a week is almost inevitably to have to try —
though, alas, not necessarily with success — to make oneself a poet.
For our natural insensibility there is no permanent cure. One may seek
new sights and new wonders, but that aid to awareness, like other stimulants,
must be used with caution. If the familiar has a way of becoming
invisible, the novel has a way of seeming unreal — more like a dream or a
picture than an actuality. And certainly no man is less aware of things than
the conscientious traveler who hurries from wonder to wonder until
nothing less than the opening of the heavens on judgment day would
catch the attention of his jaded brain. Madder music and stronger wine
pay diminishing returns.

   I have never practiced the swami's technique for "heightening consciousness"
and I doubt that I ever shall. For one thing, I am not sure that I
want to be so exclusively aware of either myself or the All in the colorless
essence of either. To put it in a dignified way, I prefer to live under the
dome of many-colored glass and to rest content with the general
conviction that the white radiance of eternity has something to do with it.
To put it more familiarly, what I am after is less to meet God face to face
than really to take in a beetle, a frog, or a mountain when I meet one.

My own homely technique when I walk out in my own country and realize
that I am in danger of seeing nothing at all is simply to greet each thing
as it comes along, by name if I know it: "That is a wood frog,"
"This is the caterpillar of *Papilio glaucus*," and "This is some member of the
Compositae clan I don't remember ever to have seen before." Usually,
if the thing is not too common, I stop a moment to pass the time of day
with it, much as one does with an acquaintance met on the street.
"A nice day—for frogs," I may remark pleasantly; or perhaps, "I don't think
I've seen you since last summer." The plants and animals to whom I issue
such bits of conversational small change are not any more interested
or impressed than the people to whom one says the same things, but neither
are they much less so. And in both cases the purpose achieved is much
the same. I have noticed them; sometimes they have noticed me; and I am
reminded of something which a certain kind of person is rather prone to
forget—that there are other creatures in the world beside himself.

When a white-winged dove calls across the desert, it no longer sounds owl-like or sinister, and it is dovelike because I now know the dove which utters it. But I do still hear it and I still take it in.

This is an ideal sort of awareness, the kind one would have always if one could. Perhaps, indeed, there are a few individuals who do live continuously with it. But one has some doubts when one notices how regularly even those who most desire it put back into some past the happy time when it was really theirs.

Says Wordsworth:

> There was a time when meadow, grove, and stream,
> The earth, and every common sight
> To me did seem
> Apparell'd in celestial light,
> The glory and the freshness of a dream.

"*In youth*, before I lost any of my senses," says Thoreau, "I can remember that I was all alive." But in Thoreau's case also, it was "once" and not "now" that he had experienced in simple life joys such "as might inspire the muse of Homer and Shakespeare."

At least, both Wordsworth and Thoreau knew that when the light of common day seemed no more than common it was because of something lacking in them, not because of something lacking in it, and what they asked for was eyes to see a universe they knew was worth seeing. For that reason theirs are the best of all attempts to describe what real awareness consists of, and for an opposite reason Walter Pater's is certainly the fussiest, if not actually the worst. Surely no one ever succeeds for long in burning "with a hard and gemlike flame" if his method is the method recommended by the inventor of that dubious phrase. When he advises us to stalk, as it were, exquisite sensations, and seems to warn us how alert we must be if we are not to miss one of those special moments when something or other in nature, or art, or music is reaching perfection, he talks as though only a few things were worth experiencing. How unlike Wordsworth and Thoreau, who realized that the rare moment is not the moment when there is something worth looking at but the moment when we are capable of seeing.

Elephant trees, near Santa Catarina

I shall not delude myself into thinking that at this moment the fauna and flora of the desert are "coming to perfection." I know that if they seem fascinating and beautiful it is because I am ready to look, not because they are more ready than always to be looked at. And as a guide to life I like better than Pater's fussiness the hearty exclamation of Yorick:

"'Lord!' said I, '—What a large volume of adventures may be grasped within this little span of life, by him who interests his heart in everything, and who, having eyes to see what time and chance are perpetually holding out to him as he journeyeth on his way, misses nothing he can *fairly* lay his hands on.'"

Every schoolboy knows—or at least has been told—that our ignorant ancestors believed in "spontaneous generation." They assumed of course that all the nobler animals, including man, had to have a mother and, usually, a father as well. But the humbler creatures were so little different from the mud and slime amidst which they lived that they were assumed to be merely generated by corruption. Hence, so it seemed, some organism was taking every day the great step from lifelessness to life.

Food kept too long turned into maggots. Thousands of creepers and crawlers were generated every year when the waters of the Nile receded. "Out of strength cometh forth sweetness," said Samson—because he had seen the carcass of a lion that had apparently rotted itself into a colony of bees.

The assumption died hard. Late in the eighteenth century common sense was still defending it hotly, and one need not be surprised. Life is very persistent and very ingenious in seizing every opportunity.

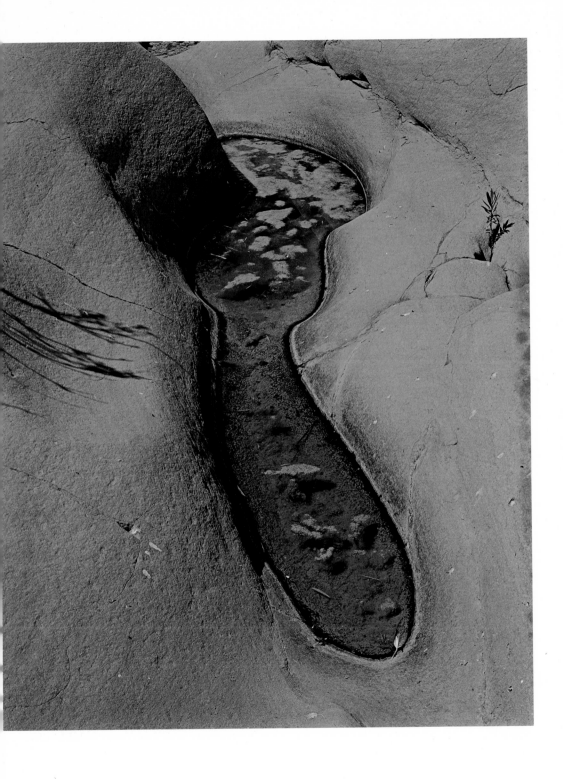

On the bare rocks of high mountain peaks flourish the lichens which,
even some of the more sceptical astronomers now admit, might grow in the
atmosphere of the planet Mars. In Wyoming, the stone basins of the
scalding hot springs are bright with yellow algae. In the almost saturated
brine of the Great Salt Lake, a shrimp which cannot live unless thus
dreadfully pickled passes his presumably happy life. And it is in the
sandiest parts of the White Sands that the yucca sends down its forty-foot
root while pale, sand-colored rodents dig about its base.

    A lichen is an admirable organism. It is the first colonizer of bare rock,
and it can live where nothing else can. It has, if I may be so impudent
as to put it this way, my great respect. Mars seems a trifle less bleak when I
think that lichens may grow there. The thought of a dead universe
is harder to bear than the thought of one in which green scales expand and
grow a little before they die.

Stones and red lichen, near San Ignacio

In desert country everything from the color of a mouse or the shape
of a leaf up to the largest features of the mountains themselves is more likely
than not to have the same explanation: dryness.

So far as living things go, all this adds up to what even an ecologist
may so far forget himself as to call an "unfavorable environment." But like
all such pronouncements this one doesn't mean much unless we ask
"unfavorable for what and for whom?" For many plants, for many animals,
and for some men it is very favorable indeed. Many of the first two
would languish and die, transferred to some region where conditions were
"more favorable." It is here, and here only, that they flourish. Many men
feel healthier and happier in the bright dry air than they do anywhere else.
And since I happen to be one of them, I not unnaturally have a special interest
in the plants and animals who share my liking for just these conditions.

Agaves, road to Bahía de los Angeles

After all, few environments are entirely favorable. No one out in a
blizzard or ice storm in southern New England is likely to think of it as
calculated to coddle man, beast or vegetable. For months in a New England
winter, every living thing has been on the desperate defensive; most have
temporarily given up the struggle and are lying low. A great many
will never revive from the inanition into which they have sunk. In the desert,
heat and drought are no more difficult to survive. Some of the
techniques of survival are different, some are surprisingly similar to those
which are used to cope with cold.

We human beings are not very rugged as living organisms go. In fact we are
extraordinarily tender creatures who can exist even uncomfortably
only within a very narrow range of temperature and only if protected from
most of the manifestations of nature. In the New England winter we warm
ourselves with fires and if we go out we bundle ourselves up in wool
or even in rubber to ward off cold and dampness. We think it nothing
extraordinary to stay all day in the house because the weather is a little
more unfavorable than usual. In the desert the only difference is that the
inclemencies from which we protect ourselves are different. If we tend to keep
out of the sun in midsummer, occasionally even stay in the house
almost all day because it is too hot to go out, inhabitants of the so-called
temperate regions are compelled even more frequently to keep out of the
cold and the wet. Actually we are considerably less at the mercy of the
elements than they are.

Men of most races have long been accustomed to speak with scorn of the
few peoples who happen to live where nature makes things too easy.
In the inclemency of their weather, the stoniness of their soil, or the rigors of
their winter they find secret virtues so that even the London fog has
occasionally found Englishmen to praise it. No doubt part of all this is
mere prejudice at worst, making a virtue out of necessity at best. But
undoubtedly there is also something in it. We grow strong against the pressure
of a difficulty, and ingenious by solving problems. Individuality and character
are developed by challenge. We tend to admire trees, as well as men, who bear
the stamp of their successful struggles with a certain amount of adversity.

Fig tree, road to Punta San Francisquito

Geology seems to demonstrate that the earliest flowering plants depended, as the conifers do today, upon the chance that some of their abundant pollen would be carried by the wind to the waiting ovaries. Then, since all organic matter is potentially edible by something, it is assumed that certain insects got into the habit of eating pollen, accidentally got some of it entangled in the hair on their bodies as many still do, and accidentally rubbed some of it off on the stigmas of the other flowers they visited. Since, for the plant, this was more effective than wind pollination and involved less waste of vital material, those plants which were most attractive to insects got along best. And as the degree of attractiveness accidentally varied, "natural selection" favored those which were most attractive, until gradually all the devices by which plants lure insects or birds — bright colored petals, nectar which serves the plant in no direct way, and perfume which leads the insect to the blossom; even the "guide lines" which sometimes mark the route to the nectar glands —were mechanically and necessarily developed.

Gardeners usually hate "bugs," but if the evolutionists are right, there never would have been any flowers if it had not been for these same bugs. The flowers never waste their sweetness on the desert air or, for that matter, on the jungle air. In fact, they waste it only when nobody except a human being is there to smell it. It is for the bugs and for a few birds, not for men, that they dye their petals or waft their scents. And it is lucky for us that we either happen to like or have become "conditioned" to liking the colors and the odors which most insects and some birds like also. What a calamity for us if insects had been color blind, as all mammals below the primates are! Or if, worse yet, we had had our present taste in smells while all the insects preferred, as a few of them do, that odor of rotten meat which certain flowers dependent upon them abundantly provide. Would we ever have been able to discover thoughts too deep for tears in a gray flower which exhaled a terrific stench? Or would we have learned by now to consider it exquisite?

Hedgehog cactus in bloom

Agave and mist, south of Rancho Rosarito

The whole story, as it is usually told, of how flowers developed is thus a rather tall tale, as indeed the whole story of evolution is. That two different organisms should have simultaneously adapted themselves one to another is, if I understand the laws of probability, at least four times as improbable as that one should have adapted itself to the other. I am not saying I don't believe it did. On the whole I think I do, at least with one reservation. But sometimes I can't help saying to myself, "A man who will believe that will believe anything."

This world would be a far less interesting as well as a far less varied place,
if every problem which faces either plants or men was always solved
in the same way. Thoreau remarked that he would like to have as many
different kinds of men as possible. Fewer and fewer seem to agree with him.
But it certainly looks as though nature wanted as many different kinds
of living things as she could produce. And she pursues her love of
variety even down to the smallest detail. If one beetle has twelve spots,
she is pretty certain to make another with fifteen—and she is almost
as profuse in the desert. Water storage in a thick stem works very well not
only for the saguaro but also for the great and very common barrel cactus,
which, as I have said before, really does hold enough water in its pulp to save
a human life in desperate cases. But that is no reason why gourds
and the queen of the night shouldn't go in for underground tubers instead.
Thus nature:

> . . . *fulfills herself in many ways*
> *Lest one good custom should corrupt the world.*

Barrel cactus, near San Agustín

All the methods of keeping water, once one has got it, are variations
of the same one, namely, a method of preserving a high ratio of mass to
surface. That means thick, succulent leaves (if any); stems which
store up moisture, and which also often serve the purpose of leaves —
since leaves are too lavish in their evaporation to be afforded by some
desert plants. The cactus, of course, is the plant which seems most typical
of these devices. Its thick, watery stem bears no leaves at all and,
being green all over because of the chlorophyll distributed over its whole
surface, the stem can everywhere manufacture the body-building materials
which it is the function of the leaves to produce in a normal plant.

But by my side, nobody.
Only the desert: cactus, thornbushes, huge rocks bursting beneath
the sun.
Cricket not singing . . .
and the air would have broken in a thousand pieces if anyone had
shouted: Who's there?
Stripped hills, cold volcano, stone and hot wind under all that
splendor, drought, the taste of dust,
a barefoot sound in the dust, and a peppertree in the midst of desert
like a petrified fountain!

Cardon cactus, road to Punta San Francisquito

As for the plants which neither send roots deep nor practice conservation
so conspicuously, they choose to riot briefly and then lie low, either as seeds
waiting for their short weeks of life or, sometimes, as dry roots or
shriveled stems hoping for a rainy day. For the most part they are small,
like the herbaceous plants of a garden, and they burst suddenly into a riot of
blossom. It is they which are chiefly responsible for the desert's
sensational spring, and it must be strangely like that of the arctic, where the
shortness of the warm season produces the same result as the shortness
of the wet one. In both regions the plants rush from bud to seed with
astonishing rapidity. Of the prudence, the foresight, and the thrift of the
paloverde or the cactus these desert prodigals seem to know little and care less.
"*Carpe diem*" and "We're a long time dead" are their guiding principles.
But, like their human analogues, they are responsible for a good deal of the
color and gaiety of their world.

Thistle poppies, near El Arco

As for the animals, some of them drink when they get a chance; and I have caught sight of the commonest of the little lizards darting his tongue two or three times into the water of a small ditch dug to irrigate a cultivated shrub. Nevertheless, many of the rodents seldom drink, since they depend largely upon the moisture in the plants they eat. Others never drink at all; and there are a few which never even eat any food not bone-dry. Theirs is the ultimate ingenuity; and one needs to be a chemist to understand how they do it, for without ever taking in any moisture at all they nevertheless give some out and their veins continue to run blood, not sand.

The key to the riddle is the fact that water is composed of hydrogen and oxygen and that these elements, otherwise combined into carbohydrates, exist in the starch of even the dryest seeds the never-drinking rodent eats. In the laboratory of his digestive system he breaks these carbohydrates down, and by recombining two of the elements he makes for himself the water he must have. For that feat he deserves, I think, to be called the desert dweller par excellence and to rank, as an example of just how far nature will sometimes go, just a little above the boogum tree (*Idria colunaris*) which is certainly the oddest specimen of desert flora, as he is the oddest of the fauna.

One finds the boogum wild only in Lower California. If I had not seen it with my own eyes, I should not believe it, for it is far more improbable looking as a tree than the giraffe is as an animal. Whether it was christened by some admirer of Lewis Carroll or whether some accident of convergence is responsible for the fact that even the gravest botanical treatises call it by a name which occurs elsewhere only in *The Hunting of the Snark*, I do not know. In any event, the name is gloriously appropriate because the boogum tree looks far more like something out of *Alice* or the *Snark* than like any real tree. Speaking of the strawberry, Dr. William Butler, a worthy who was one of Shakespeare's contemporaries, made the sage remark: "Doubtless God could have made a better berry but doubtless God never did." Doubtless He could have also made a queerer tree than the boogum, but if He did I have never heard of it.

What one sees when one undertakes to contemplate it is an inverted, green-barked cone, six or eight feet high and with the proportions of a carrot. The general effect is rather like a large taproot that has for some reason grown up into the air instead of down into the earth. From this cone scattered twigs a few inches long project foolishly in all directions. At some seasons a few futile leaves dangle from these twigs, though they were bare when I saw them. Only another Lewis Carroll word will do to describe it; like the borogoves in *Alice*, it is "mimsy" —which, as Humpty-Dumpty explained, means both flimsy and miserable.

So inelegant a solution of a problem is seldom achieved or at least seldom persisted in by Nature, who may not be infallible but who has buried most of her mistakes in geologic time, where this one ought to have been forgotten along with some of the equally inadvisable animals who had their regrettable day. The essayist Charles D. Stewart once analyzed the orthodox tree "as an invention," but he did not mention this one which, so far from being a credit to the inventor, looks like one of those unbelievable triumphs of no ingenuity exhibited by the patent office in hopes of raising a smile. To see three of these vegetable monstrosities together — and three together I have seen, one like a chunky carrot, the other two foolishly elongated —is to suspect that some of nature's journeymen had made trees and not made them well, they imitated an organism so abominably. If the time ever comes when the desert no longer seems to me at all strange, I know how I shall remind myself that it is. I shall imagine a mouse-that-never-drinks resting in the conical shade of a boogum tree.

I can understand how an astronomer may conclude that God is a mathematician. The planets seem to know where they are going and what they are about. Theirs is a formal, unvarying dance which moves in accord with an abstract scheme of delightful regularity; and the mathematical physicist seems to have discovered that the microcosm is, despite the disturbing presence of certain principles suggesting indeterminacy, a good deal like its big brother the system of heavenly bodies. But the world of living things exhibits no such co-operation of part with part, no such subordination of the unit to the whole. The God who planned the well-working machines which function as atom and solar system seems to have had no part in arranging the curiously inefficient society of plants and animals in which everything works against everything else; and the struggle between, let us say, the mouse which would continue its species and the owl which would feed its young goes on inconclusively millennium after millennium.

No one, it seems to me, who has ever watched the contest between two weeds for a few square inches of soil; no one who has seen all the intricate history of the one, from seed to leaf, come to nothing—can possibly suppose that so wasteful a game of cross-purposes was deliberately devised by the astronomer's mathematical God, or indeed by any intelligence which knew what it wanted. If a God made the world of atoms and suns, then perhaps life intruded itself unexpectedly to impose, through some will of its own, multiplicity upon unity, disorder upon order, conflict upon balance. The individual plant or animal is no doubt marvelously contrived to achieve its purposes, but the society of living things is an anarchy in which events may work themselves out to this conclusion or that—but over which no unity of purpose seems to preside.

Boogums, agaves, and other things, south of Rancho Rosarito

Life is rebellious and anarchical, always testing the supposed immutability
of the rules which the non-living changelessly accepts. Because the
snowflake goes on doing as it was told, its story up to the end of time was
finished when it first assumed the form which it has kept ever since.
But the story of every living thing is still in the telling. It may hope and it
may try. Moreover, though it may succeed or fail, it will certainly change.
No form of frost flower ever became extinct. Such, if you like, is its glory.
But such also is the fact that makes it alien. It may melt but it cannot die.
Like the star, the snowflake seems to declare the glory of God, while the
promise of the amoeba, given only perhaps to itself, seems contemptible.
But its jelly holds, nevertheless, not only its promise but ours also, while
the snowflake represents some achievement which we cannot possibly share.
After the passage of billions of years, one can see and be aware of the other,
but the relationship can never be reciprocal. Even after these billions
of years no aggregate of colloids can be as beautiful as the crystal always was,
but it can know, as the crystal cannot, what Beauty is.

There is something about the fern leaf which stirs us —or at least some
of us —as the frost flower cannot. We can love it in a different way —
not as pure Beauty, but with a love which is impossible without something
like sympathy or fellow feeling. And we can sympathize because we know
that the fern is like us, while the frost flower is not.

How shall we define that "something like us"? Is it merely that we are both
perishable intruders into a dead environment over which we both, temporarily
at least, are able to triumph? Or is it something still more than this?
Is it because we can say —and mean something when we say it —that the fern
"wants" to be left alone in its cranny by the rock? Certainly many people
do have some such feeling and they are right to have it. In some sense all
living things are allied in some sort of struggle against all that are not living.

Granite and boogum, road to Punta San Francisquito

I need, so I am told, a faith, something outside myself to which I can be loyal.
And with that I agree, in my own way. I am on what I call "our side,"
and I know, though vaguely, what I think that is. Wordsworth's God had his
dwelling in the light of setting suns. But the God who dwells there seems
to me most probably the God of the atom, the star, and the crystal.
Mine, if I have one, reveals Himself in another class of phenomena. He
makes the grass green and the blood red.

In the legends of the saints and the prophets, either a desert or a mountain is pretty sure to figure. It is usually in the middle of one or on the top of the other that the vision comes or the test is met. To give their message to the world they come down or come out, but it is almost invariably in a solitude, either high or dry, that it is first revealed.

Moses and Zoroaster climbed up; Buddha sat down; Mohammed fled. Each in his own way had to separate himself from men before he could discover what it was that he had to say to mankind. In a "wilderness" (Near Eastern and therefore certainly xeric) Jesus prepared himself for the mountaintop from which he would reject the world which Satan would offer. Loneliness is essential and loneliness, it would seem, is loneliest where the air is either thin or dry and nature herself does not riot too luxuriously. If Plato was satisfied with no more than a grove in Athens, that was because he was already halfway to the mere college professor.

Yesterday, when I stood on a peak and looked down at an arid emptiness, I felt on my shoulders an awful responsibility. Under such circumstances as these, said I to myself, other men have grown wise. Only a few before me have ever had the double advantage of mountain and desert. It is now or never. If *the answer* is ever to be whispered into my willing ear, this should be the moment.

No awful presence—I hasten to add—handed me any tablets of the law. Neither did Satan appear to offer me the world, and if he had done so I might, for all I can really know, have taken him up. Yet it did seem that I saw something with unusual clearness and that I came down not quite empty-handed.

From where I stood there was no visible evidence that the earth was inhabited. Like some astronomer peering through a telescope at the planet Mars, I could only say, "It might be." It was thus the world must have looked at the end of the fifth day, and I found myself wondering whether the text of Genesis might not possibly be garbled; whether, perchance, it was really after the fifth, not after the sixth day, that God looked at his work and saw that it was good. Would not I, in His place, have stopped right there? Would I have risked the addition of a disturbing element? Was the world ever again so obviously good?

Buttes and morning mist, road to San Borjas

Not to have known—as most men have not—either the mountain or the desert is not to have known one's self. Not to have known one's self is to have known no one, and to have known no one makes it relatively easy to suppose, as sociology commonly does, that the central problems are the problems of technology and politics. It makes it possible to believe that if the world has gone wrong—and seems likely to go wronger—that is only because production and distribution are out of balance or the proper exercise of the franchise has not yet been developed; that a different tax structure or even, God save the mark, the abolition of the poll tax in Alabama, point the way to Utopia. It is to forget too easily that the question of the Good Life—both the question what it is and the question how it can be found—has to do, first of all, not with human institutions but with the human being himself; that what one needs to ask first is not "What is a just social order?" or, "In what does true democracy consist?" but "What is Man?"

That question neither the usual politician, nor the usual economist, nor the usual scientist has ever asked, because he has never been alone. No man in the middle of a desert or on top of a mountain ever fell victim to the delusion that he himself was nothing except the product of social forces, that all he needed was a proper orientation in his economic group, or that production per man hour was a true index of happiness. No such man, if he permitted himself to think at all, ever thought anything except that consciousness was the grandest of all facts and that no good life for either the individual or a group was possible on any other assumption. No man in such a position ever doubted that he himself was a primary particle, an ultimate reality.

Yucca and boulder, road to Santa Catarina

Abrí los ojos, los alcé hasta el cielo y vi cómo la noche se cubria de estrellas.
¡Islas vivas, brazaletes de islas llameantes, piedras ardiendo, respirando, racimos de piedras vivas,
cuánta fuente, qué claridades, qué cabelleras sobre una espalda oscura,
cuanto río allá arriba, y ese sonar remoto del agua junto al fuego, de luz contra la sombra!
Harpas, jardines de harpas..

I opened my eyes, I looked up at the sky and saw the night covered with stars.
Live islands, bracelets of flaming islands, stone burning, breathing, clusters of live stones,
how many fountains, many brightnesses, comet-tail-hair on a dark back,
how many rivers far up there, and that remote sounding of water with fire, of light against shade!
Harps, gardens of harps.

The "fixed" stars are only relatively fixed—relative, that is, to the brief span of our own lives. "As changeless as the stars in their courses" is not really changeless and thus, though nothing else in all our experience seems so immobile as the polestar, even it also moves.

Between the time when it was first pointed out to our childish eyes and the time when, on our dying day perhaps, we will look up at it for the last time, it will not have seemed to move, no matter at what hour or what season we may look. Yet in twelve thousand years, so they tell me, it will have moved so much that Vega, which now blazes near the zenith on an autumn evening and then declines toward the west, will be where Polaris now is and will rest there, apparently immobile, while all the other stars, including Polaris itself, make their circles about it. In another twelve or thirteen thousand after that, Polaris and Vega will be back again where they now are.

This "precessionary" cycle of the equinoxes is complete in a little more than twenty-five thousand years and that is the longest cycle of recurring events about which we know anything. Yet it has fulfilled itself many times since the earth's history began and may fulfill itself many more before it ends.

Beyond the limits of that cycle, even the most learned astronomers can only guess at the meaning of a perceptible drift in the whole solar system. Is that drift part of some vaster circling which it will take even longer to complete and are we swinging through some orbit too vast to compute, or are we *really* drifting away from some point in space to which we shall never return, toward some unimaginable destination? That question is beyond even speculation. Perhaps we are following the curve of space and perhaps, after an infinity of time, we will come back again to where we now are, back from a journey which took us an infinite distance. The one thing we do know is that the most fixed of known points is not really fixed at all.

"Whither the Movies?" "Whither Democracy?" "Whither Mankind?" A thousand editorials have asked these questions. "Whither?" indeed. Meanwhile, in the Lower Sonoran Desert, the ant's granary is full.

Sunrise, Cabo San Lucas

2. A Smoother Pebble,
A Prettier Shell

OBJETOS

Viven a nuestro lado,
los ignoramos, nos ignoran.
Alguna vez conversan con nosotros.

OBJECTS

They live alongside us,
we do not know them, they do not know us.
But sometimes they speak with us.

"Up, up and quit your books" is not an adjuration commonly thought
advisable in universities, but there are occasions—as, for instance, when
studying Wordsworth—when it might be advisable. Commonly the professor
who has just finished an exposition of the poem concludes somewhat
as follows: "The assignment for next time is the next twenty pages of your
anthology and don't forget that the monthly book report is due."
Is it any wonder that students don't take poetry seriously?

All men are Peter Bell most of the time. When a yellow primrose becomes
for the scientist more than simply a yellow primrose, it is likely to be
merely Primula sp. and that is no great advance. For the student of literature
it probably remains stubbornly "A poem in four-line stanzas of iambic
pentameter by William Wordsworth (1770-1850)." What's Primula to him
or he to Primula? But sometimes the answer does come: "Everything."

Not all the techniques together—science, poetry, and mere looking—
have ever yet enabled anyone even at his happiest moments to confer
being even for one instant on more than a small fragment of all that exists.
What we should like to do—though it might blast us if we did—is to
realize the sum of the earth's energy and joy. The most we can usually do is
to participate in the opening of one flower or in a rabbit's running of his race.
There is too much beauty and too much joy for us to take in. Any man
really capable of what at moments he feels himself on the brink of
would be conscious of everything going on in the universe. He would be
both flying with the eagle and growing with the grass.

Too long a view in either time or space makes people miss a great deal that is close at hand, and it is my experience that those who are quickly bored in the country are usually those who lack "the microscopic eye," those to whom "nature" means only "scenery," and "scenery" means only "views." Charles Lamb once declared that he would not much care if he never saw another mountain, and, while I would not by any means go so far, I think I know what he meant. To know nature only that way is like knowing a city only by its skyline. To feel the life of either city or country, one must be actually in it, aware of the excitement and variety of individual lives. People are often blamed because they cannot see the wood for the trees, but that does not seem to me so bad as not seeing the trees for the wood.

Dry succulent, seashore near El Rosario

Elephant tree in bloom, El Marmolito

Landscape is not inclined to geometry. The human mind is; most living things are. They employ, as man does, the circle, the sphere, the triangle, and the star. Tree and herb alike demonstrate how stresses may be calculated and supported by struts, buttresses, and columns like those which man will use. Also, and unlike the hill or the valley, they reveal how regularity and repetition constitute the essential elements of formal design. If we did not borrow from living nature a very large part of the art of both building and design, then we, being also living things, independently discovered what the builders of branches, the designers of seed pods, the constructors of shells and bones, discovered before us.

If I were a painter or a sculptor more interested in design than in
story-telling, it seems to me that I should go instead to the living organisms.
I should go to the blossom, which usually builds up a pattern of fives
or threes; to the seed pods, which come in an infinite variety of boxes,
flasks, and urns; even, if I wanted a "mobile," to the ripe fruit of the
wild geranium, whose effective catapult was tossing hard round seeds many
millenniums before the military engineers of the Renaissance discovered
that the same principle could be used to hurl boulders at an enemy.

Even an amateur like myself will seldom lack something to see if he will only look. "Lift up thine eyes unto the hills" is a religious exhortation. "Go to the ant, thou sluggard," is a scientific one. And, at least for certain temperaments, it is the more fruitful. Because I obey it, the place where I am is never really the same place two days in succession, and I can take every morning the same short walk down a certain wood road because it is not really the same walk.

One is not compelled to remain always standing before the picture frame, or confined to the spectator's side of the proscenium. One may walk into the picture, become part of the poem, or even participate in the drama itself. From no mere canvas does the wind actually blow; there is no poem from which a snowflake can detach itself to melt upon the cheek. From every man-made poem, or picture, or drama, one is to some extent excluded. A certain separateness from it is necessary if it is to be art at all. We must contemplate and we must not intervene. But of nature's poems and pictures we are invited to become a part.

Ver, tocar formas hermosas, diarias.
Zumba la luz, dardos y alas.
Huele a sangre la mancha de vino en el mantel.
Como el coral sus ramas en el agua
extiendo mis sentidos en la hora viva

To see, to feel the lovely daily forms.
Buzzing of light, arrows, and wings.
It smells of blood, this winestain on the table.
Like the branches of coral stretched out in the water
I stretch my senses in the living hour

Desert vegetation, near Mezquital on road to Santa Rosalía

Façade, Mission San Borjas

Hills, road between Valle de la Trinidad and La Calentura

Thoreau's life was not spent either in writing or even in physically inactive
meditation but in doing the hundreds of outdoor things which he
loved to do and in actively pursuing the duties of that office—inspector of
snowstorms and rainstorms—to which he said he had appointed himself.
"I sit in my boat on Walden, playing the flute this evening, and see the perch,
which I seem to have charmed, hovering around me, and the moon
traveling over the bottom, which is strewn with the wrecks of the forest,
and feel that nothing but the wildest imagination can conceive of the
manner of life we are living. Nature is a wizard. The Concord nights
are stranger than the Arabian nights." A few years later he was writing to
one of his mystical friends: "I have sworn no oath. I have no designs on
society, or nature, or God. . . . I love to live. . . . I have heard no bad news.
. . . When you travel to the Celestial City, carry no letter of introduction.
When you knock, ask to see God—none of his servants . . .

. . . In what concerns you much, do not think that you have companions;
know that you are alone in the world."

"I wish," he wrote, on his third day beside the pond, "to meet the facts of life—the vital facts which are the phenomena or actuality the Gods meant to show us—face to face, and so I came down here." But even that was not quite all. Thoreau was still, and always remained, enough of a Transcendentalist to believe that there was also some ultimate truth beyond "phenomena" and "actuality" which could be caught only, if at all, by grace of a direct, superrational communication from nature to man. And one thing was certain: at Walden one saw more of the significant "phenomena" and "actualities" than one saw of them in a city or even in a village, and on the basis of that fact it was reasonable to suppose that, living more naturally, one was also more nearly attuned to the truth which might some day be communicated.

To a mouse which ran over his shoes and up the inside of his pantaloons he fed a bit of cheese from his fingers, feeling the comfortable assurance that "There is not much danger of the mouse tribe becoming extinct in hard winters, for their granary is a cheap and extensive one." "And then the frogs, bullfrogs; they are the more sturdy spirits of ancient wine-bibbers and wassailers, still unrepentant, trying to sing a catch in their Stygian lakes." He was sure that he was more nearly of the frogs' fellowship than he was of any fellowship gathered in towns; more a part of their ancient world than of that newer one which had created needs to which it was now enslaved. "If I am not quite right here," he wrote, "I am less wrong than before." And he was supremely happy. "Sometimes, when I compare myself with other men, methinks I am favored by the gods. They seem to whisper joy to me beyond my deserts, and that I do have a solid warrant and surety at their hands, which my fellows do not. I do not flatter myself, but if it were possible, they flatter me. I am especially guided and guarded." And again: "Every natural form—palm leaves and acorns, oak leaves and sumach and dodder—are untranslatable aphorisms."

Date palms, San Ignacio

When the young John Muir had reached the Cumberland Mountains
in the course of his "Thousand Mile Walk to the Gulf," he spent the night
with a serious blacksmith struggling to survive in the remote backwoods
of a region lately devastated by the Civil War. When he was asked
what had brought him and replied that he had come to look for plants
this dialogue ensued:

"What kind of plants?"

"Oh, all kinds; grass, weeds, flowers, trees, mosses, ferns—almost everything
that grows is interesting to me. . . ."

"You look like a strong-minded man," he replied, "and surely you are
able to do something better than wander over the country and look
at weeds and blossoms. These are hard times, and real work is required of
every man that is able. Picking up blossoms doesn't seem to be a
man's work at all in any kind of times."

To this I replied, "You are a believer in the Bible, are you not?" "Oh, yes."
"Well, you know that Solomon was a strong-minded man and he is
generally believed to have been the very wisest man the world ever saw,
and yet he considered it was worth while to study plants; not only to go
and pick them as I am doing, but to study them; and you know that we are
told that he wrote a book about plants, not only the great Cedars of
Lebanon, but of little bits of things growing in the cracks of the walls.

"Therefore you see that Solomon differed very much more from you than
from me in this matter. I'll warrant you he had many a long ramble in the
mountains of Judaea, and had he been a Yankee he would likely have
visited every weed in the land. And again, do you not remember that Christ
told his disciples to 'consider the lilies how they grow,' and compared their
beauty with Solomon in all his glory? Now whose advice am I to take,
yours or Christ's? Christ says 'Consider the lilies.' You say 'Don't consider
them. It isn't worth while for any strong-minded man.'"

Cardon cactus and blooming bush, road to Santa Rosalía

Muir may have been a bit sportive in citing his Biblical examples, but his predecessors were not. Nature, so they thought, was what Sir Thomas Browne had called it, "the art of God." To consider the lilies was to consider His work and therefore an act of worship. Not to consider them was to be contemptuously indifferent toward what He had created for man's admiration. And not even the humblest living thing failed to declare His glory since, as an ancient patriotic writer had said, "He created in heaven the angels and in the earth, worms; nor was He superior in the one case or inferior in the other. If no other hands but His could create the angels, neither could any other create the worms."

When the young Thoreau proclaimed in his graduation address that "this curious world which we inhabit is more wonderful than it is convenient; more beautiful than it is useful . . . more to be admired and enjoyed than used," he was saying precisely what the modern world most emphatically does not believe. But like Muir he was consciously or unconsciously echoing what had once been the premise of the old naturalists who were less intent upon "useful knowledge" than upon the discovery of what John Ray, England's first great naturalist, was to call "The Wisdom of God Manifest in the Works of the Creation." "Let us then," he wrote, "consider the Works of God and observe the operations of his hands. . . . No creature in the sublunary world is capable of so doing, besides man, and yet we are deficient herein."

The nineteenth century was deeply concerned with what it called
"man's place in nature," and as some of the writers pointed out, that had
much more than merely scientific implications. It did not imply only,
or even most importantly, that man was descended from the apes and was,
therefore, still apelike in many of his characteristics. It meant also that
animal life supplied the inescapable context of his life, spiritually as well as
physically. It meant that life was an adventure which he shared with all
living things, that the only clue to himself was in them. But of that fact
many, perhaps most, of the most intelligent and cultivated people of our time
are unaware. Having to do almost exclusively with other human beings
and with machines, they tend to forget what we are and what we are like.
Even the graphic arts are forsaking nature so that even on the walls of
our apartments the wheel or the lever are more familiar than the flower or the
leaf. And perhaps all this is the real reason why we have tended more
and more to think about man and society as though they were machines,
why we have mechanistic theories about consciousness and about human
behavior in general, why we have begun to think that even the brain is
something like an electronic calculating machine. After all, it is only
with machines that most people are more than casually familiar. And perhaps
it is trying to think in this way that makes us unhappy —nearly everybody
seems to agree that we are —because we know in our hearts that we are not
machines and grow lonesome in a universe where we are little aware of
anything else which is not.

Pero también las piedras pierden pie, también las piedras son
imágenes,
y caen y se disgregan y confunden y fluyen con el río que no cesa.
También las piedras son el río.

Beauty and joy are natural things. They are older than man, and they have
their source in the natural part of him. Art becomes sterile and the joy of life
withers when they become unnatural. If modern urban life is becoming
more comfortable, more orderly, more sanitary, and more socially conscious
than it ever was before—but if at the same time it is also becoming less
beautiful (as it seems to me) and less joyous (as it seems to nearly everyone)—
then the deepest reason for that may be its increasing forgetfulness of nature.
She is often none of the good things which the city is, but she is almost
always, nevertheless, somehow beautiful and somehow joyous.

   Joy is the one thing of which indisputably the healthy animal, and even the
healthy plant, gives us an example. And we need them to remind us
that beauty and joy can come of their own accord when we let them.
The geranium on the tenement window and the orchid in the florist's shop,
the poodle on the leash and the goldfish in the bowl, are better than nothing.
In the consciousness of the city-dweller, they ought to play a part no less
essential than that of the sleek chrome chair and the reproductions of
Braque and Miro.

Stones also lose their footing, stones too are images,
and they fall and they scatter and mix and flow with the flowing
river.
The stones also are the river.

Palo Blanco, road to San José de Comondú

Here I have, literally, God's plenty. Everything reminds me that man is an incident in nature rather than, as one comes to suppose in the city, that the natural is, at most, an incident, surviving precariously in a man-made world. If I do on my own a little of that peeping and botanizing which Wordsworth scorned, I think that I profit less from what I learn *about* nature than I do from what I should prefer to call the example she sets me — the example, I mean, of confidence, of serenity, and, above all, of joy. In the city, perhaps especially in the city of today, one may pass whole weeks without meeting a single joyous person or seeing a single joyous thing. One may meet laughter there, and wit — sometimes, perhaps, a fragment of wisdom. These are all good things which I would not willingly do without. But joyousness, as distinguished from diversion and amusement and recreation, is so rare that a whole philosophy has been developed to make a virtue out of its absence.

The world, we are told, is a terrible place, and it is wicked not to be almost continuously aware of the fact. Diversion in limited quantities is permissible as a temporary relaxation, but moral indignation should be the staple of any human life, properly spent. Yet it seems to me that Joy and Love, increasingly fading from human experience, are the two most important things in the world, and that if one must be indignant about something, the fact that they are so rare is the thing most worthy of indignation.

Granite and bush, Sierra de Juarez

Unfortunately the scientific study of living creatures does not always promote either reverence or love, even when it is not wholly utilitarian in its emphasis. It was the seventeenth-century naturalist John Ray who first gave wide currency in England to the conviction that God made other living things not exclusively for the use of man but also for both his delight and for theirs.

Unfortunately that laboratory biology which has tended to become the most earnestly cultivated kind of scientific study is precisely the kind least likely to stimulate compassion, love, or reverence for the creatures it studies. Those who interested themselves in old-fashioned natural history were brought into intimate association with animals and plants. Its aims and its methods demanded an awareness of the living thing as a living thing and, at least until the rise of behaviorism, the suffering and the joy of the lesser creatures was a part of the naturalist's subject matter. But the laboratory scientist is not of necessity drawn into any emotional relationship with animals or plants and the experiments which of necessity he must perform are more likely to make him more rather than less callous than the ordinary man.

Very recently I had occasion to spend a week on the campus of one of the oldest and most respected of the smaller liberal arts colleges of the eastern seaboard. It was one that prides itself on its exclusive concern with liberal rather than preprofessional education. A benefactor gave it some years ago a beautiful wooden tract adjoining the campus which is lavishly planted with native and exotic flowering trees and shrubs. When no student or teacher with whom I had been brought into contact could tell me the name of an especially striking tree, I sought out the head of the botany department, who was also its only member.

He smiled rather complacently and gave this reply to my question: "Haven't the least idea. I am a cytologist and I don't suppose I could recognize a dozen plants by sight." The secrets of the cell are a vastly complicated and important subject. But should they be the one and only thing connected with plant life which a student seeking a liberal education is given the opportunity to learn?

Ocotillo peninsularis, Vizcaíno Desert

To pick up even what Newton called "a smoother pebble or a prettier shell than ordinary, whilst the great ocean of truth lay all undiscovered before me" one usually needs nowadays to be a specialist, and even within the limits of one science the specialist must specialize. He is a zoologist or a botanist or a cytologist or a biochemist and if he is a botanist he limits himself to the ferns or the fungi, the grasses or the flowering plants; and even then he may be regarded by the real specialists as inclined to spread himself rather thin.

Once when I was window-shopping in a side canyon of the Catalina Mountains I met a stranger who turned out to be the greatest living authority on the ants of the United States. Noticing my binoculars he amiably told me that he had seen some interesting-looking birds not far away. "What were they?" "Oh, I don't know the names of any birds. In fact I try not to know any. There are so many ants that it is all I can do to remember them."

92]

And there is one such I shall never forget.

His specialty was water beetles and he came to Baja on the assumption that just because there wouldn't be many water beetles there it would be especially valuable to know about those that were—the next best thing, indeed, to being a specialist in the snakes of Ireland. While all the other members of the expedition permitted themselves to enjoy the scenery (even if they were not geologists) and to admire the flowers (even though they were not botanists) this dedicated young man dozed in complete silence with only one eye open until a puddle appeared. Then he would spring to life, give an agonized shout to the driver of the truck, and leap out with net, collecting bottles, and whatnot. I am sure that he will in time know all about water beetles but I wonder if he will know much about anything else. Perhaps a kindlier reaction would be that of the late, great spoofer of naturalists, Mr. Will Cuppy, who wrote:

"Here is the place, by the way, to mention those herpetologists who specialize in garter snakes. Herpetologists are people who know all about snakes and other reptiles, also amphibians. They are like other people, except that they are herpetologists. By counting the dorsal scales and the labial, ventral and subcaudal scutes, studying the stripes, and measuring the tails of thousands and thousands of garter snakes, they have succeeded in dividing the little fellows into a number of species and subspecies; more, to be candid, than actually exist. For each new species he discovers, the herpetologist receives a bonus.

"Yet herpetologists have their place in the scheme of things. Because of them, we know that Butler's garter snake has, in most instances, only six supralabials, a state of affairs caused by the fusion of the penultimate and antepenultimate scutes. We who take our garter snakes so lightly may well give a thought to the herpetologists counting scutes on the genus *Thamnophis* in museum basements while we are out leading our lives. Most of the specimens are pickled."

Ocotillo and no water beetles, Las Arrastras de Arriola

Many specialists are very contemptuous of such activities as mine —
but not all of them are. Some steal time from their exacting pursuits to be
amateurs at something else or even, like me, of things in general.
Thus they recapture some of the spirit of the old naturalists who, whether
they were professionals like Linnaeus or hobbyists like Gilbert White,
lived at a time when there seemed nothing absurd about taking all nature as
one's province. And there are even some, eminent in their specialty,
who experience a certain nostalgia for the days when the burden of
accumulated knowledge was less heavy. "The road," said Cervantes,
"is always better than the inn" and discovering is more fun than catching up
with what has been discovered.

Los ojos ven, las manos tocan.
Bastan aquí unas cuantas cosas:
tuna, espinoso planeta coral,
higos encapuchados,
uvas con gusto a resurrección . . .

Eyes see, hands touch.
A few things are enough:
prickly pear, the coral and thorny planet,
the hooded figs,
grapes tasting of resurrection . . .

Columnar cactus, near Rancho Arenoso

. . . and clams, stubborn virginities,
salt, cheese, wine, bread of the sun.
From her high darkness an island girl looks at me,
a slim cathedral clothed in light.
Towers of salt, seen by the shore's green pines,
the white sails of the boats rise up.
Light builds its temples on the sea.

. . . almejas, virginidades ariscas,
sal, queso, vino, pan solar.
Desde lo alto de su morenía una isleña me mira,
esbelta catedral vestida de luz.
Torres de sal, contra los pinos verdes de la orilla
surgen las velas blancas de las barcas.
La luz crea templos en el mar.

Your amateur is delightfully if perhaps almost sinfully free of responsibility
and can spread himself as thin as he likes over the vast field of nature.
There are few places not covered with concrete or trod into dust where he
does not find something to look at. Best of all, perhaps, is the fact that he feels
no pressing obligation to "add something to the sum of human knowledge."
He is quite satisfied when he adds something to *his* knowledge. And if
he keeps his field wide enough he will remain so ignorant that he may do
exactly that at intervals very gratifyingly short.

3. Strange Gods

Unos me hablaban de la patria.	*Some spoke of our land.*
Mas yo pensaba en una tierra pobre,	*But I thought of a poor earth,*
pueblo de polvo y luz,	*people of dust and light,*
y una calle y un muro	*a street and a wall*
y un hombre silencioso junto al muro.	*and a silent man up against the wall.*
Y aquellas piedras bajo el sol del páramo	*And those stones in the clear upland sun*
y la luz que en el río se desnuda . . .	*and light standing naked in the river . . .*
olvidos que alimentan la memoria,	*forgotten things that feed my memory,*
que ni nos pertenecen ni llamamos,	*irrelevant things, not summoned up,*
sueños del sueño, súbitas presencias	*dreams of a dream, those sudden presences*
con las que el tiempo dice que no somos,	*with which time tells us that we have no being,*
que es él quien se recuerda y él quien sueña.	*that time is the one who remembers and who dreams.*
No hay patria, hay tierra, imágenes de tierra,	*There is no country, there is earth and its images,*
polvo y luz en el tiempo . . .	*dust and light living in time . . .*

The way of the desert and the way of the jungle represent the two opposite methods of reaching stability at two extremes of density. In the jungle there is plenty of everything life needs except mere space, and it is not for the want of anything else that individuals die or that races have any limit set to their proliferation. Everything is on top of everything else; there is no cranny which is not both occupied and disputed. At every moment, war to the death rages fiercely. The place left vacant by any creature that dies is seized almost instantly by another, and life seems to suffer from nothing except too favorable an environment. In the desert, on the other hand, it is the environment itself which serves as the limiting factor. To some extent the struggle of creature against creature is mitigated, though it is of course not abolished even in the vegetable kingdom. For the plant which in the one place would be strangled to death by its neighbor dies a thirsty seedling in the desert because that same neighbor has drawn the scant moisture from the spot of earth out of which it was attempting to spring.

Sometimes it seems to me that, of the two methods, the desert's is the kindlier and that, though I have never seen the jungle, it is there rather than here that I should feel the sense of discomfort (or worse) which the desert produces in some of those who experience it for the first time. Certainly I am little aware of any such discomfort. I wonder if it does not augur ill for the human race that its techniques have enabled it to produce for itself a sort of artificial, technological jungle in which too many people can live somehow —if not well—and where, therefore, as in the jungle, the struggle inevitably becomes ultimately the struggle of man against man and not the struggle of man against nature.

Barrel cactus, near San Agustín

Whenever men stop *doing things* long enough to *think about them*, they always ask themselves the question: "What am I?" And since that is the hardest of all questions to answer they usually settle for what looks easier—"If I don't know what I am, then can I tell what I am like?"

To that there are three common answers: "Like a god," "Like an animal," and "Like a machine." Perhaps there is some truth in all but the most evidently true is the second.

Man does not know how much he is like a god because he does not know what a god is like. He is not as much like a machine as he nowadays tries to persuade himself, because a machine cannot do many of the things he considers of supreme importance. It cannot be conscious; it cannot like, dislike, or desire. And it cannot reproduce its kind.

But man is so much like an animal—which can do all these things— that even the most convinced proponents of the other two answers always admit that he is something like an animal too.

Primitive man acknowledges the likeness by adopting an animal "totem," and by inventing legends which recall a time when the community was closer and more openly manifest.

Granite boulders, Laguna Hans

Believing that everything about him was alive, primitive man attributed a psychic life to mountains and winds, to rivers and stones. No doubt the distinction that was slowly made between the living and the inanimate was tremendously important in defining his own mental world, because it tended to draw him emotionally closer to other living things while it marked him off from whatever did not live. But it is a curious aspect of modern intellectual development that modern thought has, on the contrary, tended to obliterate again the distinction, to interpret life in mechanistic terms until, by now, it might almost be said to have come to a conclusion exactly opposite the assumption of primitive man. If the latter thought that everything in the universe was alive, the mechanist believes that nothing is, and the significance of even the word "organism" as distinguished from the word "machine" tends to disappear. Moreover, and as the result of a somewhat similar development, the medieval man who saw "purpose" everywhere and, for the most part, purpose directed toward him and his needs, has given way to the mechanist who sees purpose nowhere and rejects the assumption of even the most generalized "intention" in nature almost as vehemently as he rejects a naïve, man-centered teleology.

The paradox of Man, who is part of nature yet can become what he is only by being also something unique, is so desperate that it never has been, perhaps never can be, resolved, and it is likely to lead those who ponder it from one foolish extreme to another. Wordsworth notwithstanding, Nature is quite capable of betraying the heart that loves her. But if she is not dependably the Kind Mother neither is she as (Tennyson was already calling her in pre-Darwinian days) always "red in tooth and claw." By our standards she is sometimes the one; sometimes the other. Her processes do not correspond exactly to any set of values we formulate. We must say of her only that she is what she is, sometimes what we wish her to be, sometimes repugnant to us. We both admire and are repelled. We co-operate and we resist. We dare not follow her blindly. But neither can we afford not to learn from her. She is magnificent and inscrutable. We are what Pope called us two centuries and a half ago, "The glory, jest and riddle of the world." We face back toward our primitive ancestors, perhaps even to the ape; we also look forward to we know not what. Ambiguous creatures that we are we can neither be satisfied with nature nor happy unless we achieve some compromise with her.

Grave and wreath, San Ignacio

"How right was Darwin?" I asked, and I answered: "Only partly."
Natural selection, which operates only to perpetuate that which has survival
value, can account for much. But it cannot account for the intensification of
consciousness. If nature has a tendency, if she "wants" anything, it is
not merely to survive. It is to realize more completely the potentialities
of protoplasm. Of the "why" we may, as Wheeler said, be always ignorant
and of the "how" we may never know more than a very little. But the
evolutionist himself has spread before us a story from which it seems to me
impossible not to draw the conclusion that there is some drive toward
"the higher," not merely toward that which has the best chance of survival.

But if man is the "highest" animal yet to appear, then—it may be asked—
is there anything to be gained by preserving indefinitely the links in the chain?
Are all other creatures "lower" and therefore to be regarded as merely
something which has fulfilled its function? If so, then is the only reason for
preserving them that we can use them as objects of curiosity, perhaps learn
something useful from them about our own physiology, or even get from
them some consolation for what would otherwise be our loneliness?

There is, so it seemed to me, also something else. In our rise to
our human state we have lost something despite all that we have gained
by becoming so largely intellectual, so persistently given to the questions
"why" and "for what purpose." We often call our lives "a rat race";
but did any rat ever think of his own existence in such terms?

Rocks and vegetation, near El Mármol

Is it a merely sentimental delusion, a "pathetic fallacy," to think that one sees in the animal a capacity for Joy which man himself is tending to lose? I do not think it is. We have invented exercise, recreation, pleasure, amusement, and the rest. To "have fun" is a desire often expressed by those who live in this age of anxiety. Most of us have experienced the desire and most of us have at times actually "had fun." But recreation, pleasure, amusement, fun, and all the rest are poor substitutes for Joy; and Joy, so I at least am convinced, has its roots in something from which civilization tends to cut us off.

Are some at least of the animals capable of teaching us this lesson of Joy? Some biologists deny categorically that they feel it. But by no means all and by no means the best. If I listen to a cardinal singing outside my window as I write I am convinced. The gift for real happiness or joy is not always proportionate to intelligence as we understand it, even among the animals. As Professor N. J. Berrill has put it: "To be a bird is to be alive more intensely than any other living creature, man included. Birds have hotter blood, brighter colors, stronger emotions... They are not very intelligent... but they live in a world that is always the present, mostly full of joy." Similarly Sir Julian Huxley, certainly no mere sentimental "nature lover," wrote after watching in Louisiana the love play of herons who, with loud cries of ecstasy, twine their necks into a lover's knot: "Of this I can only say that it seemed to bring such a pitch of emotion that I could have wished to be a heron that I might experience it."

La hora es transparente:
vemos, si es invisible el pájaro,
el color de su canto.

The time is transparent:
even if the bird is invisible,
let us see the color of his song.

Yellow blossoms, Punta Gasparino

We talk about conquering nature, planning society, even of "intervening in the process of evolution." But we should remember the exclamation of Archimedes, "Give me a fulcrum for my lever and I can move the earth," and what we should note most carefully is the fact that a fulcrum must lie outside the thing itself. We cannot move our world unless there is something outside that world which we believe to be solid and immovable.

Unless we know what ought to be done as well as how to do this or that, we become merely skillful technicians without wisdom—which is precisely what we now are. We do not ride, we are ridden. The machines we have made control us. The ancients had a good motto: "Quo Urania ducit"— Wherever Wisdom leads. Ours has become instead: "Quo Uranium ducit."

¡Dia, redondo día,
luminosa naranja de veinticuatro gajos,
todos atravesados por una misma y amarilla dulzura!

Albert Einstein once told the students at the California Institute of Technology
that he doubted whether present-day Americans were any happier than the
Indians who were inhabiting the continent when the white man first came.
Not many are likely to agree with so extreme a statement but quite
a few, I think, would admit that, leaving the Indians out of it, we are not
as much happier than our grandfathers as it would seem our gains in health,
security, comfort, convenience, as well as our release from physical pain ought
to make us. Does this failure to pay off have something to do with a
misjudgment concerning what man really wants most or, at least, a failure
to take into account certain of the things he wants besides comfort,
wealth and the rest?

By 1980, they say, you will be broiling steaks in electronic stoves,
owning a two-helicopter garage and, of course, looking at television in
full color. These assurances are supposed to make it easier for the housewife
to put up with mere electric ovens, ninety-mile-an-hour automobiles and
soap operas in black and white. From such makeshifts they are supposed to
lift sparkling eyes toward a happier future. And perhaps that is precisely
what they do do. But will they be as much happier as they now think
they inevitably must be? Is it really what they want? Is the lack of
these things soon to come chiefly responsible for the irritations, frustrations
and discontents they now feel?

Suppose they were promised instead that by 1980 the world in which
they live will be less crowded, less noisy, less hurried and, even, less
complicated. Suppose they were told that they will have more opportunities
to see the beauties and to taste the pleasures of sea and mountain and stream,
to have more contact with the wonders of trees and flowers, the abounding life
of animal creatures other than human. Would the prospect look even brighter?

Day, round day,
luminous orange with twenty-four sections,
all saturated with one single yellow sweetness!

Sunrise, Mulege

Henry Thoreau put the feelings of a minority better than they will ever be able to put it for themselves: "I spend a considerable portion of my time observing the habits of the wild animals, my brute neighbors. By their various movements and migrations they fetch the year about me. . . . But when I consider that the nobler animals have been exterminated here — the cougar, panther, lynx, wolverine, bear, moose, deer, the beaver, the turkey, etc., etc., —I cannot but feel as if I lived in a tamed and, as it were, emasculated country. Would not the motions of these larger and wilder animals have been more significant still? Is it not a maimed and imperfect nature that I am conversant with? As if I were to study a tribe of Indians that had lost all its warriors. Do not the forest and the meadow now lack expression, now that I never see nor think of the moose with a lesser forest on his head in the one nor of the beaver in the other? When I think what were the various sounds and notes, the migrations and works, and changes of fur and plumage which ushered in the spring and marked the other seasons of the year, I am reminded that this my life in nature, this particular round of natural phenomena which I call a year, is lamentably incomplete. I listen to a concert in which many parts are wanting. The whole civilized country is to some extent turned into a city, and I am that citizen whom I pity. . . . Primitive Nature is most interesting to me. I take infinite pains to know all the phenomena of spring, for instance, thinking that I have here the entire poem, and then, to my chagrin, I hear that it is but an imperfect copy that I possess and have read, that my ancestors have torn out many of the first leaves and grandest passages, and mutilated it in many places. I should not like to think that some demigod had come before me and picked out some of the best of the stars. I wish to know an entire heaven and an entire earth."

Ocotillo and rock, Las Arrastras de Arriola

The discovery of America meant different things to different people. To some it meant only gold and the possibility of other plunder. To others less mean-spirited it meant a wilderness which might in time become another Europe. But there were also not a few whose imaginations were most profoundly stirred by what it *was* rather than by what it might become.

The wilderness and the idea of the wilderness is one of the permanent homes of the human spirit. Here, as many realized, had been miraculously preserved until the time when civilization could appreciate it, the richness and variety of a natural world which had disappeared unnoticed and little by little from Europe. America was a dream of something long past which had suddenly become a reality. It was what Thoreau called the great "poem" before many of its fairest pages had been ripped out and thrown away. The desire to experience that reality rather than to destroy it drew to our shores some of the best who have ever come to them.

Bunch grass and an elephant tree, near Santa Cata

Thomas Henry Huxley, improving on a hint from Darwin, once propounded
a sort of riddle. The prosperity of the farmer's clover crop depends,
so he said, upon the number of old maids in the British Isles.
Pretty farfetched, you think. Actually, not so much so as you can be
forgiven for supposing. The explanation goes like this: Clover blossoms
set seed only if they have been fertilized by bumble bees—which need to be
very abundant. Field mice eat the larvae of bumble bees, but cats cut
down the number of field mice. Old maids are notoriously prone to
keep cats. Ergo, the more old maids, the more cats; the more cats, the fewer
field mice; the fewer field mice, the more bumble bees, and the more
bumble bees, the more clover. . . .

Man, who likes to think that only his welfare and indeed only his tastes
should count, is inclined to regard all such arrangements as unnecessarily
complicated. Since he is mildly pleased by trees, he doesn't see why
it is necessary to have caterpillars to eat them and then sawflies to keep down
the caterpillars. Why not just have no caterpillars to begin with? Nature's
scheme seems rather too much like that of the old man's in *Alice:*

> But I was thinking of a plan
> To dye one's whiskers green
> And always use so large a fan
> That they could not be seen.

Why dye them green in the first place?
On man's own egotistical assumptions the question is a good one.
But he is the only creature who makes it, and he might as well face the fact
that "Nature's children all divide her care." Perhaps man is her most
remarkable achievement. But perhaps also—as some mystic might suggest—
she is less concerned about him than about some of her others, now that
he has so confidently taken things into his own hands and boasts
that at last he is "conquering nature." Obviously, she prefers her own
system of balance in which cougars as well as deer and caterpillars as well as
aspens and sawflies all flourish. Why? Is it because she loves variety
for its own sake or because it is by the endless variety of her experiments
that she has brought life to its present state of development and that she
intends to go on with the experimentation, giving each creature a chance to
see what it can make of itself?

Succulent, near Rancho Arenoso

An obviously unfriendly reporter revealed not long ago that President Eisenhower had ordered removed from the White House lawn the squirrels which were interfering with his putting green, and even so trivial an incident is a straw in the wind. To hold golf obviously more important than squirrels indicates a tiny but significant decision. It points toward a coming world where there will be more golf courses and fewer wild plants as well as wild animals — hence to a world less interesting and less rich for those who would rather hunt a flower or watch the scamperings of a squirrel than chivy a rubber ball over a close-cropped grass plot.

The late David Fairchild, who was responsible for the introduction of so many useful and beautiful plants into the United States, tells the story of an army officer assigned to an office building in Miami during the First World War.

"I haven't got anything but human beings around me in that building where I spend my days. Aside from the floor and the ceiling, the doors and windows and desk and some chairs there isn't anything but people. The other evening when I was feeling particularly fed up with the monotony of the place, I went into the laboratory and as I was washing my hands a cockroach ran up the wall. 'Thank God for a cockroach!' I said to myself, 'I'm glad there is something alive besides human beings in this building.'"

It may well be with such small consolations that the nature-lover of the not too distant future will be compelled to content himself. Cockroaches will not easily be exterminated.

Lava and bleached bush, near San Ignacio

Some years ago Mr. Clifton Fadiman used—and for all I know may have invented—the phrase "the failure of attention." Nearly everyone seemed to recognize its aptness. It covered everything from the schoolteachers' complaint that children would no longer take the trouble to learn arithmetic, to the publishers' discovery that "condensations" sold better than original masterpieces and that pictures which could be glanced at were increasingly preferred to essays which had to be read.

The college student plays the radio while he studies because he cannot keep his mind on his books; vacationers at the beach take along a phonograph, a deck of cards, and various other pieces of paraphernalia because neither the sea itself nor any one of their other diversions can hold them for long.

Kelp, Santa Catarina Landing

What philosophers used to call "the good life" is difficult to define and impossible to measure. In the United States today—increasingly also in all "progressive" countries—we substitute for it "the standard of living," which is easy to measure if defined only in terms of wealth, health, comfort, and convenience. But the standard of living does not truly represent the goodness of a life unless you assume that no other goods are real.

No one could call either the few scattered inhabitants of Baja's open country or those who inhabit La Paz, its southern metropolis, "affluent." Here is an economy, not of abundance, but of desperate scarcity, where food and water are hard to come by and manufactured goods so scarce that "use up and make do" are not a philosophy but an inescapable necessity, and most things that cannot serve their original purpose any longer are made to serve some other. No one there is likely to be able to understand what is meant by the necessity for an advertising art to "create needs" or by the dangers of "underconsumption."

That one meets there smiling children and seemingly contented men may seem to prove that theirs is to some degree a good life. "Swept and garnished" is the phrase which sums up, not only La Paz, but all except the most forlorn of the villages. Though chickens may wander around palm-thatched huts there is no dismal accumulation of trash like that which disgraces almost every American community. In La Paz the buildings may be in need of repair but they are not frowzy—only resigned, so it seems, to the inevitable decline which a clean old man accepts. . . .

With us, advertisers solemnly congratulate themselves upon their success in "creating needs"; there, even minimal needs are hard to satisfy. There, to revert again to abstraction, is an economy of almost unqualified scarcity; here, one of almost unqualified abundance. . . .

Corral and blue palms, Arroyo Catavina

Because of that stark fact, men not only live differently and act differently; they also think and feel differently. Here we seek excuses to discard, replace, and throw away. We are a little ashamed to use up or wear out; indeed we are sometimes told that to do so is to threaten with disloyalty the very prosperity which makes it possible to have more than we need. But it will be a long time before the inhabitants of Baja are able to grasp even as an abstraction the concept of "psychological obsolescence." "Use up" and "make do" are more than merely necessary habits; they are moral injunctions.

When some physical object can no longer serve the purpose for which it was first intended there is nearly always something else for which it can be used. The automobile which has been repaired until it can be repaired no more supplies spare parts for another one not quite so far gone and, indeed, may serve with gradually reduced efficiency in one vehicle after another. Thus, "made" things return to the earth by a series of stages somewhat like those by which the body of a man, once the most complex of machines, is reduced step by step to simple inorganic chemicals, his protoplasm feeding first, perhaps, some lower animal, then some vegetable growth, then the bacteria of decay, and thus becomes successively protein, an amino acid and, at long last, merely carbon, calcium, and phosphorus again. Similarly machines, tools, and even bottles and boxes disintegrate in Baja as they serve simpler and simpler uses. The hood of a no longer usable car becomes the roof of the lean-to or part of one side of a shack; the empty soup can grows an ornamental plant; the bottom of a broken bottle outlines a flower bed; the discarded tire serves as the sole of a sandal and has become, I believe, an article of commerce.

A century ago the naturalist, Xantus, complained that he could find no boxes in which to ship his specimens because the few which turned up in Baja were quickly seized and made into furniture. Times have not changed as much as one might expect. In the wilds near a small village I saw boys digging up the camp trash we had buried in order to salvage tin cans. In La Paz itself the humbler housewives carefully avoid crushing the shells of the eggs they eat in order that these shells may be sold for an infinitesimal fraction of a cent to merchants who stuff them with confetti and then sell them again to the revelers at Mardi Gras who delight to break them finally over one another's heads.

Shrine, road along Bahía de la Concepción

It is true that the literary man as spokesman and prophet does not stand very high today even among the more educated classes. Any contemporary *Heroes and Hero Worship* would have to put the Hero as Man of Letters low in the hierarchy and the Hero as Man of Science at the top. But suppose we turn to these modern heroes. From some of the best of them you will get cold comfort. Here, for instance, is J. Robert Oppenheimer:

"Nuclear weapons and all the machinery of war surrounding us now haunt our imaginations with an apocalyptic vision that could well become a terrible reality: the disappearance of man as a species from the surface of the earth. It is quite possible. But what is more probable, more immediate and in my opinion equally terrifying is the prospect that man will survive while losing his precious heritage, his civilization and his very humanity. . . ."

But what is this "humanity" which the *Nation* is interested in and Oppenheimer fears we may lose? It is easier to say what it isn't or to define it negatively. It is that part of man's consciousness, intellect, and emotion which is neither exclusively interested in nor completely satisfied by either mere animal survival on the one hand, or wealth, power, and speed alone. It is that part of him which is least like a machine and therefore least satisfied by machines. It is the part that would like to know itself and that cherished values to which nothing in the inanimate world seems to correspond and which the nonhuman world of living things only dubiously (though none the less comfortingly) seems to encourage.

Perhaps we are being a bit provincial to call this "humanness." Man existed for many millennia without, so we guess, exhibiting much of it. Perhaps Mr. Oppenheimer is right in supposing that he might endure indefinitely after he had lost it. Many contemporary men—and especially many contemporary youths—to whom only automobiles, airplanes, and television sets seem interesting, have already lost most of it. Perhaps it is primarily a phenomenon of recent man and, in the form we best understand, of Western man. Perhaps what some of us tend to call "the human being" first came into easily recognizable existence about the year 475 B.C. and began to disappear about seventy-five years ago. But though the world may soon belong to other creatures, there are some of us who cannot say simply, "Cultures come and go," without a regret for the passing of what seems to our possibly prejudiced minds more worthy of admiration than anything which ever existed before.

Cove and mangroves, Bahía de la Concepción

If man has no true nature as distinguished from what his condition at a given
time creates; if no persisting needs, tastes, preferences, and capacities
are either met or frustrated by that condition; then there is no reason why he
should not be as contentedly "adjusted" to the condition of what
Johnson calls a "geometrician" exclusively. But if there *is* such a thing as
human nature, and if both man's history and his literature give some clue
as to what that nature is; if, indeed, they reveal it more surely than all the
polls, questionnaires and tests which "geometry" has been able to devise;
then Johnson may be right when he suggests that it is in man's nature to be
moral and, perhaps, even religious; that it is, as a matter of fact,
in accord with his nature to be a moralist perpetually and a geometer only
by chance. And if you do believe this to be true, then it may also seem
that the deepest cause of the anxiety which has given its name to our age;
that the deepest cause of the fact that man is not so secure, so happy, and so
content in his age of power and abundance as it would seem that he
should be; that he is, indeed, so frequently forced to seek the aid of
psychiatrists or those who can minister to a mind diseased that we are told
it is impossible to train as many such ministers as are now needed —
if all this is true then, it may be, I say, that the deepest reason is simply this:
Man's condition as geometer and as the child of geometry is not harmonious
with his nature.

Even most of those who are neither Christian nor, in any ordinary sense, mystical do nevertheless feel that there is something lacking in our society and that this lack is not generally acknowledged; do feel that, for all its prosperity and for all its kindliness, generosity, and good will, it is somehow shallow and vulgar; that the vulgarity is superficially evidenced in the tawdriness, the lack of dignity and permanence in the material surroundings of our lives, and more importantly in our aims and standards; that we lack any sense that efficient and equitable systems of production and distribution are only a beginning, as, for that matter, are also our ideal of democracy and our struggle for social justice. You may, as a few do, attribute this alienation to "a lack of religion." But perhaps even that term is not broad enough. It is a lack of any sense of what life is *for* beyond comfort and security, and it would still be so even if all these good things were conferred upon all. At best life would still remain, in Yeats' phrase, "an immense preparation for something which never happens."

A very popular concept today is embodied in the magic word cybernetic —
or self-regulating. "Feedback" is the secret of our most astonishing machines.
But the famous balance of nature is the most extraordinary of all cybernetic
systems. Left to itself it is always self-regulated. The society we have
created is not, on the other hand, cybernetic at all. The wisest and most
benevolent of our plannings requires constant attention. We must pass this or
that law or regulation, then we must redress this balance of production
and distribution, taking care that encouraging one thing does not
discourage something else. The society we have created puts us in constant
danger least we ultimately find ourselves unable to direct the more and
more complicated apparatus we have devised.

A really healthy society, so Thoreau once wrote, would be like a healthy
body which functions perfectly without our being aware of it. We, on the
other hand, are coming more and more to assume that the healthiest society
is one in which all citizens devote so much of their time to arguing,
weighing, investigating, voting, propagandizing, and signing protests in a
constant effort to keep a valetudinarian body politic functioning in some sort
of pseudo-health that they have none of that margin for mere living
which Thoreau thought important.

Platitudes, like folk songs, are usually anonymous. Even when they come into fashion during some remembered hour of history, the credit or the blame can seldom be assigned to an individual man. But, as everybody knows, it was Lord Acton who said, "All power tends to corrupt; absolute power corrupts absolutely." And that has become, among intellectuals, one of the most familiar of platitudes.

We accept it as true of both individuals and governments. No man and no organization can, we believe, be trusted with unlimited or even with very great power. He or it may be virtuous to begin with but will do ill in the end. Power is both evil and the cause of evil. Men cannot be like gods because they will become devils instead.

Strangely enough, however, what we assert of individuals, of governments, of groups, and even of nations, we do not believe of mankind itself. We look with suspicion on the individual who has risen too high; we devise checks and balances designed to limit economic groups and political parties; very recently we have begun to urge nations to limit their sovereignty voluntarily. But we still rejoice in every addition to the power which mankind as a whole can exercise and never assume that it also might become a victim of *hubris*.

Men have spent a great deal of time wishing they were angels. Cats, dogs, and the rest never seem to wish they were anything else. To some this is lack of ambition. But should we, perhaps, call it contentment instead? The two are often terribly difficult to tell apart.

Elephant trees, near Rancho Rosarito

Up to the present, mankind may have profited more than it has suffered from the various powers it has been able to exercise. Let us assume that it has. But that is, at best, no more than good luck. At no moment has it ever known or, indeed, seriously considered what the consequences were likely to be. What actually happens when the steam engine or the dynamo or, for that matter, the automobile, the airplane, and the radio, is invented is simply this: Our hearts lift up and we let out a glad cry, "Hold on to your hats boys, here we go again."

Even if it is assumed that more good than evil has always resulted so far, the results have certainly not all been unqualifiedly good. There was a time when the whole question of the industrial revolution hung in the balance. For a generation it enslaved children and they were freed just in the nick of time —i.e., just before child slavery could become an accepted social institution. At the present moment millions of children instead of standing in front of looms are seated in a seemingly milder enslavement before "giant twenty-one-inch screens," hypnotized by distant and usually anonymous masters who find it profitable in one way or another when certain images, sounds, and reiterated statements are presented to the eyes and ears of their victims.

It was nothing like this which Marconi, De Forest and the rest intended. Neither was it the enslavement of children nor the creation of poisonous smog clouds that Watt intended. But all these things were among the direct consequences. Who knows how this generation of children is to be set free?

Pacific shore, north of El Rosario

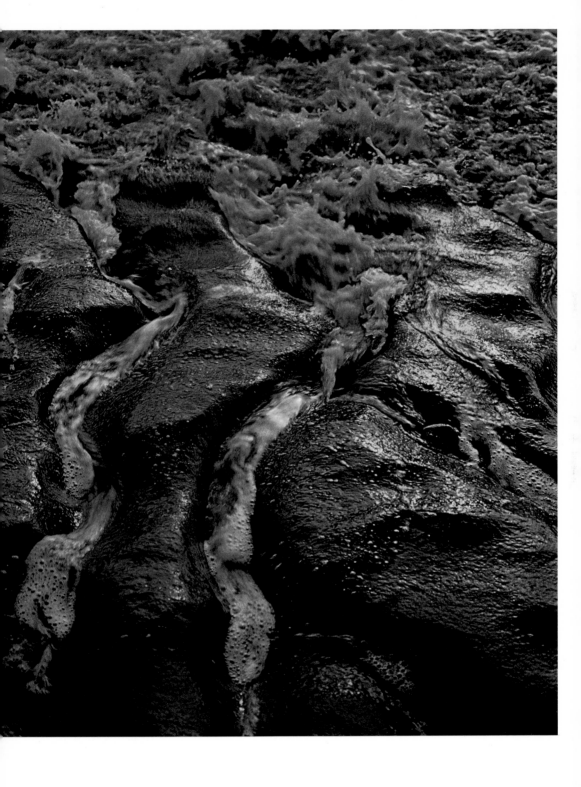

Since the beginning of the scientific age, there have been differing conceptions of what science was "for." Quite properly it was sometimes regarded as "useful" and sometimes as valuable simply because it increased understanding. But though pure science is a legitimate pursuit, pure technology) i.e., technology regarded as an end in itself) is antihuman — and it is to that we have come. The machine rather than man has become the measure of all things and we regard the improvement, even the welfare, of man's tools as more important than man's own.

We are no longer much surprised when we hear, for example, that a rocket expert who designed weapons for one of our enemies shrugs his shoulders when asked to work for us instead. He is not interested, we say, in politics. But that is not quite adequate. Actually, he is simply not interested in what rockets are to be used for. He is interested simply in rockets — which is to say in machines (or power) for its own sake. And though this attitude is only occasionally so dramatically revealed, millions have unconsciously adopted it. If we worshiped only the machines which *make* things, we might say that we were materialists. But we are almost equally impressed by those which merely *do* things —which go faster, or higher, or farther. We do not, like a utilitarian, ask what good they are or, like a materialist, what we can get out of them. Like the members of many primitive religious cults, we are uncertain whether the powers we worship are evil or good; we are sure only that they are powerful and that, therefore, they should be worshiped.

Since man first recognized or suspected power outside himself, he has worshiped many strange gods, adored them in many strange rituals and sacrificed himself to them in many strange ways. He has slaughtered animals and maidens; he has whipped, starved, and mutilated himself. He has slept on nails, gazed at the sun until blind, and held his arms aloft until they withered. It was not himself but the god of his idolatry whom he was determined to serve. And so it is again with us. To Thoreau, the inhabitants of his own Concord "appeared to be doing penance in a thousand remarkable ways." What would he think of the new ways devised since his time?

In the Sanskrit Panchatantra, that collection of romantic tales written down in an early century A.D., there is a fable which might have been devised for today. Three great magicians who have been friends since boyhood have continued to admit to their fellowship a simple fellow who was also a companion of their youth. When the three set out on a journey to demonstrate to a wider world the greatness of their art they reluctantly permit their humble friend to accompany them, and before they have gone very far, they come upon a pile of bones under a tree. Upon this opportunity to practice their art they eagerly seize. "I," says the first, "can cause these dead bones to reassemble themselves into a skeleton." And at his command they do so. "I," says the second, "can clothe that skeleton with flesh." And his miracle, also, is performed. Then, "I," says the third, "can now endow the whole with life."

At this moment the simpleton interposes. "Don't you realize," he asks, "that this is a tiger?" But the wise men are scornful. Their science is "pure"; it has no concern with such vulgar facts. "Well then," says the simpleton, "wait a moment." And he climbs a tree. A few moments later the tiger is indeed brought to life. He devours the three wise men and departs. Thereupon the simpleton comes down from his tree and goes home.

There is no more perfect parable to illustrate what happens when know-how becomes more important than common sense —and common sense is at least the beginning of wisdom.

Palms, road from Loreto to San Javier

Our prophets often describe the "new world" which lies just ahead when atomic power has been harnessed to peaceful uses; when we can travel across space instead of merely through air; or even when the work week has been reduced to twenty-five hours. But there is in actual fact nothing really *new* about this new world. It would be merely one which had taken another step in the direction which many previous steps had taken. New worlds never were and never will be created except by new ideas, or aims, or desires, or convictions. Christianity created a new world and so did the seventeenth century's new faith that a knowledge of the laws of nature could change rapidly and radically mankind's condition. To some slight extent our own age is still part of the new world Christianity created and it is still very much part of the new world which faith in science created. But there will be no newer world as long as there is no idea or ideal newer than that of the seventeenth century.

If we should ever decide that we do want a new world we shall have to find first the faith which could make it. As long as we believe that the only human reality is the human condition there will be no fundamental change in that condition. If we should become convinced again that man has a nature and that the greatest of his needs is to create a condition suited to it, then a really new world might come gradually into being.

Un silencio de aire, luz y cielo.
En el silencio transparente
el día reposaba:
la transparencia del espacio
era la transparencia del silencio.
La inmóvil luz del cielo sosegaba
el crecimiento de las yerbas.
Los bichos de la tierra, entre las piedras,
bajo una luz idéntica, eran piedras.
El tiempo en el minuto se saciaba.
En la quietud absorta
se consumaba el mediodía.

A silence of air, light, and sky.
In this transparent silence
day was resting:
the transparency of space
was silence's transparency.
Motionless light of the sky was soothing
the growth of the grass.
Small things of earth, among the stones,
under identical light, were stones.
Time sated itself in the minute.
And in an absorbed stillness
noonday consumed itself.

Barrel cactus, near Rosarito

4. One Spring Again

A través de la noche urbana de piedra y sequía
entra el campo a mi cuarto
Alarga brazos verdes con pulseras de pájaros,
con pulseras de hojas.
Lleva un río de la mano.
El cielo del campo también entra,
con su cesta de joyas acabadas de cortar.

Across the city night of stone and drought
the country comes into my room.
It reaches out green arms whose bracelets are birds
whose bracelets are leaves.
Takes by the hand a river.
The sky of the country comes in too
with his basket of jewels freshly-gathered.

"¿No tienes sangre ya? ¿Por qué te mientes?
Mira los pájaros . . .
El mundo tiene playas todavía
y un barco allá te espera, siempre."

"No blood in your veins? Why lie?
Look, the birds . . .
The world is there with its beaches
and far out there's a ship waiting for you, forever."

One trouble with the city is that there is so much bad weather there.
Nearly everybody admits that snow is merely an expensive nuisance, and
even the early summer rains serve no real purpose where there is nothing to
be watered and where sewers have to be built to drain the insipid
liquid away. Some day, no doubt, when we have become thoroughly
urbanized, whole areas will be roofed over and the ideal amount of ultraviolet
supplied by electricity. Children can be taken occasionally to the country
to see what the sun looks like as they are taken now to see a hill or a
mountain. Probably many of them will not want to go anyway, for the
country will be to them only what it was to the London club man:
"A damp sort of place where all sorts of birds fly about uncooked."
But that will be all right too—for those who like it.

The good thing about the country is, on the other hand, that we don't have
there any bad weather at all—only a number of different kinds of good.
In fact I should be willing to maintain that there, and there only, do we have
what has any right to be called weather at all—as distinguished, I mean,
from those mere inclemencies of one kind or another.

Lava flow and volcano, Las Virgenes Volcanes

Mary Austin called this the Land of Little Rain and that is better than "desert." Even her phrase is negative; it stresses what the country does not have rather than what it does. Land of Much Sunshine, might almost do. It has at least the advantage of seizing upon an indubitable fact. Land of Too Much Sunshine some might call it; but it is not, for a while at least, too much for those of us who have seldom had enough.

On the brightest and warmest days my desert is most itself because sunshine and warmth are the very essence of its character.

In this country "inclemency" means heat. One is "sunbound" instead of snowbound and I have often noticed that the psychological effect is curiously similar. It is cozy to be shut in, to have a good excuse for looking out of the window or into oneself. A really blazing day slows down the restless activity of a community very much as a blizzard does in regions which have them. Without the one or the other any society, I imagine, would become intolerably extroverted. Where there is either, a sort of meteorological sabbath is usually observed even by those who keep no other.

I have not even—and I do not need—a plan. So far as the grand events are
concerned they will be planned for me. I am no chanticleer burdened
with the belief that I have to do something to make the sun rise.
Neither am I a druid convinced that it would not turn northward again in
March if I did not implore it to do so. All such events will be taken
care of by the most reliable of functionaries and the show will go on.
The trees will bud, the grass turn green, and the hummingbird return
from Central America where I have never been but to which he repairs
every autumn. The liberal theologians of the seventeenth century said that
God caused all these things to happen in order that man should admire
His prowess and His wisdom. The less liberal nineteenth century said,
through the mouth of Ernest Renan, that He arranged the whole spectacle,
including the human subplot, for His own amusement. Even if this
second view is correct I have at least received a complimentary ticket
entitling me to a good seat and I don't intend to miss the show.

As for the minor events, I shall just let them happen. I have no project
to work on, no special subject to ponder. But in past years projects have
never failed to suggest themselves and subjects for pondering never failed to
pop up. To the best of my ability I shall play the amateur biologist
and philosopher as the occasion demands. If I see something, think something,
or remember something which strikes me as communicable and likely to be
even one-tenth as interesting to others as it has been to me I shall write it down.

The inner voice has whispered too many different things to too many different men for me to have any conviction that it is always right or that it comes from anywhere except merely from within. But some voices one must listen to, and when this voice speaks to me its authority, however little it may be, is at least as great as the authority of the latest editorial in the latest weekly or monthly review. The hardest facts, as Havelock Ellis once remarked, are the facts of emotion. Joy and love, for example, cannot be doubted when one feels them. I know that they existed *in* me and *for* me when I heard the first peepers of spring and when I watched spring turn to summer. I cannot regret that I did so. I hope that whether the rest of the world is headed toward success or failure in its largest enterprises, I shall be permitted to watch with equal satisfaction at least one spring come again.

Giant yucca in bloom

I happen to be one of those, and we are not a few, to whom the acute awareness of a natural phenomenon, especially of a phenomenon of the living world, is the thing most likely to open the door to that joy we cannot analyze. I have experienced it sometimes when a rabbit appeared suddenly from a bush to dash away to the safety which he values so much, or when, at night, a rustle in the leaves reminds me how many busy lives surround my own. It has also come almost as vividly when I suddenly saw a flower opening or a stem pushing out of the ground.

But what is the content of the experience? What is it that at such moments I seem to realize? Of what is my happiness compounded?

First of all, perhaps, there is the vivid assurance that these things, that the universe itself, really do exist, that life is not a dream; second, that the reality is pervasive and, it seems, unconquerable. The future of mankind is dubious. Perhaps the future of the whole earth is only somewhat less dubious. But one knows that all does not depend upon man, that possibly, even, it does not depend upon this earth. Should man disappear, rabbits may well still run and flowers may still open. If this globe itself should perish, then it seems not unreasonable to suppose that what inspires the stem and the flower may exist somewhere else. And I, it seems, am at least part of all this.

God looked upon the world and found that it was good. How great is the happiness of being able, even for a moment, to agree with Him.

Pebbles and kelp, Pacific shore